Write or call for our free catalog.
Bristol Publishing Enterprises, Inc.
P.O. Box 1737, San Leandro, CA 94577
(800)346-4889; in California (510)895-4461

THE JUICER BOOK II

Joanna White

BRISTOL PUBLISHING ENTERPRISES, INC.
San Leandro, California

A Nitty Gritty® Cookbook

Printed in the United States of America.

ISBN 1-55867-050-5

Cover design: Frank Paredes
Cover photography: John Benson
Food stylist: Suzanne Carreiro
Illustrator: Joan Baakkonen

CONTENTS

INTRODUCTION

In my juicer books I want to stress some very important points. Use your juicer daily! Don't let this be just a passing fad, but a way of life — part of your daily routine. Keep your juicer on the counter where you can use it easily. We all have great intentions of eating more fruits and vegetables, and we may eat an occasional token salad — but have we really made a significant change in our eating habits? Juicing is an excellent way to get fast, good nutrition to make up for the donuts, hamburgers and French fries we have a tendency to gulp down between appointments.

The nutritional and health information in this book is not meant to be the answer to all your health problems. I have personally tried many of the juice combinations for my own health and have had wonderful results. But I am more interested in simply helping people get better nutrition, and hope that these recipes will lead you on this path.

Please look in the appendices, pages 146 through 167, for valuable information: yields of juice from produce, to help you shop for the right amounts of produce for these recipes; growing seasons for produce; caloric, vitamin and mineral contents of produce; and finally, a chart of "nature's pharmacy," listing health problems and foods that may help.

Besides juice recipes, I have included recipes that utilize fresh juices and the pulp left from juicing. The pulp does not contain the major amount of nutrients, but is full of fiber and some flavor, so why not add it to your favorite recipes and reap the benefits. Apple is added to many of the vegetable juice recipes to make them more palatable. So juice, be healthy and enjoy!

DRINKS AND PUNCHES

FRUIT SLUSHY

Servings: 4

By using this technique but changing the type of juice, you can come up with virtually endless varieties of drinks. Save your ripe bananas, peel them, cut them into about 1-inch slices and freeze them in baggies so that you can use the bananas in drinks later on.

1 cup fresh orange juice
½ cup fresh strawberry juice
1 frozen banana
2 cups ice

Using a blender or food processor, process ice until it is crushed. Then mix in remaining ingredients and blend until thick and smooth. If your juice is too thick, dilute with additional fruit juice, water or even sparkling water until the desired consistency is attained. Garnish with a piece of fruit that you used in the drink and serve immediately.

PINEAPPLE GRAPE SPARKLE

Servings: 2

This is a sweet, natural juice, great for people who are anemic or have problems with digestion or arthritis.

½ cup fresh pineapple juice
½ cup fresh grape juice

1 cup sparkling water (or citrus-
    flavored natural sodas)

Slice pineapple into pieces to fit in your feed tube including the peel (if not planning to use the pulp in cooking). Push grapes into feed tube including stems and seeds. Add sparkling water to taste. If desired, lemon juice adds zip.

GRAPEAR

Servings: 2

I've found that pear is a delicious drink on its own, but sometimes needs to be diluted because it is so thick. Grape juice is a good combination with pear.

1½ cups fresh grape juice
½ cup pear juice (use firm pears)

1 tbs. fresh lemon juice (with peel)

Juice grapes with stems and seeds. Juice pear with stems and seeds. Juice lemon with peel. Taste and adjust the amount of lemon juice to your personal preference.

FRUIT COMBO

Servings: 2

Sometimes when you're using citrus fruits, the juice may have a tendency to be a little bitter because of using the pithy white part. The pith is very important because it contains so many of the nutrients, so I use either apple or grapes to sweeten the juice to make it much more palatable.

½ cup fresh orange juice
½ cup fresh grapefruit juice
½ cup fresh pineapple juice
½ cup fresh grape juice, or to taste

Remove peel from orange, but leave pith on, and juice. Remove peel from grapefruit, but leave pith, and juice. Juice pineapple with peeling. Juice grapes with stems and seeds. Mix all together, taste and adjust sweetness to your personal preference by increasing grape juice if necessary.

TROPICAL SMOOTHIE

Servings: 2

Vary fruits to make endless varieties of smoothies. A small amount of coconut cream adds a tropical taste. This drink is high in vitamin C, potassium and bromelain.

1 cup fresh strawberry juice
1 cup fresh pineapple juice

1 frozen banana, sliced
¼ cup canned coconut cream

Juice strawberries with hulls. Juice pineapple with peeling. In a blender or a food processor, process frozen banana until it is mashed; add fruit juices. Add coconut cream to taste.

SEA SIREN

Servings: 2

Sometimes when I'm serving a tropical meal I like to begin with an exotic drink. I've found this to be a favorite with my guests.

6 oz. fresh pineapple juice
6 oz. guava juice, fresh or canned
6 oz. light rum

3-4 oz. grenadine
1½ cups crushed ice

Juice pineapple with peel. Add remaining ingredients and process until smooth. Pour into tall chilled glasses. Garnish with pineapple wedges, orchids or mint leaves.

GINGER APPLE

I find ginger root to be very refreshing and spicy at the same time. This drink is particularly good for digestion and the gall bladder.

1 cup fresh apple juice   1-inch piece ginger root
1 cup fresh pineapple juice

Juice pineapple with peeling. Next juice ginger root and follow with an apple in order to facilitate ginger root going through the machine. Taste and adjust to your personal preference by adding additional apple if the ginger is too hot or increasing the ginger root if you like it a little more spicy.

SPARKLING CITRUS WATER

Whenever I'm feeling really thirsty, I find that by adding lemon or lime to my water I can quench my thirst. Lemon is wonderful for digestion and high in vitamin C.

1 tbs. fresh lemon or lime juice   8 oz. sparkling water or flavored sodas

Simply juice lemons or limes with peels. Add to taste to a plain sparkling water, tonic water or lightly flavored soda.

BLUEBERRY GRAPE JUICE

Servings: 2

Blueberries are very low in sugar and are good for pancreas problems. Grapes are excellent for anemia and ginger root is particularly good as a colon and gall bladder cleanser, so how could you possible go wrong with this drink!

1 cup fresh blueberry juice
1 cup fresh grape juice
½ cup fresh apple juice
1-inch ginger root
1 cup sparkling water or flavored natural soda

Push blueberries through juicer, stems and all. Juice grapes with stems. Juice ginger root and then push apple through to help facilitate the harder ginger root. Mix all juices together with sparkling water and taste, adding additional apple for sweetness or additional ginger root for spiciness.

FRUITED WATER REDUCER

Whenever I'm having a lot of trouble with water retention and want a sweet drink, I try this combination and it works wonders.

½ fresh cranberry juice
1 cup fresh watermelon juice, with rind
½ cup fresh pear juice
½ cup fresh apple juice

Push cranberry through juicer with watermelon pieces. It is important to include the rind because it contains so much of the nutrition and value to your health. Juice pears alternately with apple because pears are usually a little too soft to go through a juicer by themselves. Taste. Due to the tartness of the cranberries you may need to increase apple juice a little.

VEGETABLE WATER REDUCER

Asparagus, parsley and cucumber are all good natural diuretics. I add apple and carrots for natural sweetness and also to reduce a little bit of the potency of this so that it doesn't shock your system.

3-4 asparagus stalks
1 tbs. parsley juice
½ cup cucumber juice
¼-½ cup carrot juice
½ cup apple juice, or to taste

Simply feed the whole asparagus stalk down the feed tube. Wad parsley into a ball and press through feed tube until you obtain about 1 tbs. of juice. Juice cucumbers with skin and seeds. Push carrots down feed tube, large end first, and follow with apple pieces that include stems and peelings. Taste and increase apple juice to make it more sweet if desired.

CALCIUM COMFORTER

For those of you who worry about osteoporosis, you need to consider vegetables that have both calcium and vitamin K in them. Vitamin K helps the body to absorb calcium and these particular vegetables contain quantities of both these nutrients.

handful of alfalfa sprouts
½ cup cabbage juice
½ cup carrot juice
1-inch piece ginger root, juiced
¼ cup lettuce juice
½ cup apple juice, or to taste

Wad alfalfa sprouts into a ball and push down the feed tube with carrots. Juice cabbage. Wad lettuce into a ball and use apple to press lettuce through feed tube. Taste and adjust to your personal preference using additional apple juice as a sweetener if desired.

CANTALOUPE STRAWBERRY BEAUTIFIER
Servings: 2

Cantaloupe and strawberries are excellent for the complexion and also taste extremely good together. Consider adding either sparkling water for zip or some nonfat plain yogurt to give it a creamy texture.

1 cup cantaloupe juice, with peeling   ¼-½ cup water (to dilute)
¾ cup strawberry juice

Juice cantaloupe with peeling and seeds (flavor is much more intense if the peeling is included with the cantaloupe). Juice strawberries with hulls. Dilute with water if desired.

CRANAPPLE JUICE
Servings: 2

You can actually make your own cranapple juice and have all of the nutrients without the sugars, artificial sweeteners and possible preservatives. Cranberries are ideal for urinary problems.

1½ cups fresh apple juice   ½ cup cranberry juice

Juice apples with stems and skins. Juice cranberries. Taste and adjust the sweetness to your personal preference.

IRON BUILDER

When you're feeling like your energy is low or if you are possibly anemic consider these vegetables, which are high in iron.

1/4 cup fresh beet juice, with peelings
1 tbs. parsley juice
1/4 cup bean sprout juice
1/4 cup watercress juice
1/2 cup carrot juice
3/4 cup apple juice

Wash beets, cut into small pieces and push down the feed tube. Wad parsley into a ball and press down with pusher in a tapping motion. Juice bean sprouts. Wad watercress and tap down feed tube using carrots. Juice apples with skins and stems. Taste and adjust to your personal preference for sweetness, increasing or decreasing apple juice.

BEET RED

I don't usually use anything but apple with vegetables but I have found on occasion that lemon is a nice addition and does not seem to upset my stomach.

1 whole beet
4 golden delicious apples, juiced

¼ lemon, juiced

Wash beet but do not peel; cut into small pieces and juice. Juice apples with peelings and stems. Juice lemon with peeling (adjust the quantity of lemon to your personal taste).

VEGGIE HAIR HELPER

Servings: 2

These particular vegetables are especially good for hair follicles.

¼ cup alfalfa sprout juice
⅓ cup lettuce juice
⅓ cup spinach juice

½ cup carrot juice
2 tbs. parsley juice
½ cup apple juice

Press sprouts down the feed tube with the pusher. Wad lettuce and spinach into balls and tap down feed tube with carrots. Wad parsley into a ball and push down tube with apple pieces, including stems and peelings. Add more apple juice for sweetness if desired.

PAINLESS PLEASURE

For those of you suffering from arthritis: broccoli, celery and Swiss chard are the best vegetables to use. Consider starting your morning out with pineapple and grapefruit juice and sometime during the day drink at least one glass of Painless Pleasure.

¼ cup broccoli juice
½ cup celery juice
¼ cup Swiss chard juice
½ cup carrot juice
½ cup apple juice

Simply cut broccoli small enough to fit into feed tube and push down. Cut celery into about 3-inch chunks (fiber can sometimes be hard to process so you need to cut this into small pieces) and press down feed tube. Wad Swiss chard into a ball and tap down feed tube with pusher, or use carrots. Juice apple with stems and skin. Increase apple juice to your personal preference if you wish the drink to be sweeter.

MONDAY MORNING TONIC

For those that over indulge in drinking on the weekends, this particular drink helps the liver to get rid of those nasty toxins.

¼ cup green bean juice
½ cup cabbage juice
¼ cup radish juice

½ cup tomato juice
½ cup apple juice

Simply push each one of these vegetables down the feed tube to juice. Juice apple last, adjusting quantity to your personal taste for sweetness.

TASTY TUMMY TAMER

Servings: 2

Green pepper, cabbage, carrot, and parsley are the best digestion helpers. Use apple as a sweetner to make vegetable drinks more palatable.

½ cup green pepper juice
½ cup cabbage juice
½ cup carrot juice

1 tbs. parsley juice
½ cup apple juice

Cut green pepper into strips and juice with seeds. Juice cabbage and carrots. Wad parsley into a ball and push down feed tube with apple pieces. Add more apple for additional sweetness.

DRINKS AND PUNCHES   17

TAKE A BREATHER

Servings: 2

These vegetables are a great combination for breathing problems and asthma.

¼ cup collard greens juice
½ cup broccoli juice
½ cup lettuce juice

½ cup carrot juice
½ cup apple juice

Wad collard greens into a ball and tap down the feed tube with the pusher. Follow with broccoli that has been cut into long stalks. Wad lettuce into a ball and press down tube using either pusher or carrots. Finish with apples, including stems and skins. Taste and add additional apple juice for more sweetness.

POTASSIUM PLENTY

Servings: 2

If you seem to be potassium deficient and tired of eating bananas, try this drink.

1 cup carrot juice
¼ cup spinach juice
1 tbs. parsley

¾ cup celery juice
½ cup apple juice

Cut tops off carrots and push down through the feed tube large end first. Wad spinach and parsley into balls and press down feed tube using a tapping motion. Cut celery into 3-inch pieces and push through feed tube. Add apples, including stems and skins. Taste; add additional apple for sweetness.

THE PROTECTOR

For those wanting to ward off colds and flu, this is an excellent combination. I've added quite a bit of carrot and apple juice to offset the strong garlic and onion flavors.

1 tsp. garlic juice
¼ cup kale juice
1 tbs. onion juice
1 tbs. parsley juice
2 tbs. wheatgrass juice
1 cup carrot juice
¼ cup apple juice

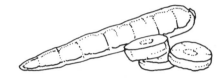

Peel garlic cloves and push down feed tube. Wad kale into a ball and push down feed tube. Peel onion, cut into pieces and press down feed tube. Wad parsley into a ball along with wheatgrass and press down feed tube with carrots or pusher. Lastly, juice apples with stems and skin. Taste and adjust to personal sweetness. You may want to add additional carrot or apple juice to tame this down a little (but keep in mind how good it is for you)!

WOMAN'S WONDER

Servings: 2

Raspberry juice is very good for menstrual cramping and women going through menopause. This is a vegetable version which also helps with P.M.S.

½ cup cabbage juice
¼ cup beet greens or collard greens juice
2 tbs. kale or okra juice
½ cup carrot juice
¾ cup apple juice
¼ cup cucumber juice

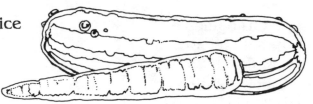

Cut cabbage into wedges small enough to feed down the tube. Wad beet greens or collard greens and use carrots to tap them down tube. Feed wadded kale or fresh okra down tube and follow with apple pieces, including skins and stems. Finish with cucumber slices, including seeds and peel. Add additional apple for sweetness if desired.

RHUBARB STIMULATOR

Rhubarb was always used as a spring tonic at our house and I never quite understood why. Now I realize that it meant "constipation reliever." And grapefruit also does the job. Because apples are used for the opposite purpose, I use grapes as the natural sweetener in this drink.

½ cup rhubarb juice
½ cup grapefruit juice
1 cup grape juice

Cut rhubarb into very small pieces and feed down the tube very slowly. (Don't force.) Peel grapefruit, leaving white pithy part, and juice. Add grapes, mixing varieties if you like, including seeds and stems. You may need to add more grape juice for additional sweetness.

CLEAR LINES

Or a better name: "Cholesterol Reducer!" Cholesterol is one of the major worries of the health conscious. Basil or mint leaves are also known to help the cause.

½ cup cabbage juice
2 tbs. parsley juice
½ cup carrot juice
4 garlic cloves (or more), peeled
½ cup green bell peppers juice, or red
½ cup apple juice
basil or mint leaves, optional

Cut cabbage into wedges to fit the feed tube, and juice. Wad parsley into balls and press down feed tube with carrots. Drop garlic cloves down tube and follow with green pepper. Finish with apple slices, including stems and peels. Add either basil or mint if in season, and taste, adjusting apple or herbs to personal preference.

SANGRIA

Servings: 4 to 6

This is a popular drink that I like to serve especially during summer. You can vary the flavor by changing the lemon to lime juice but this is the standard recipe for Sangria.

1 quart red wine
1½ cups fresh orange juice
¼ cup fresh lemon juice
1 cup sugar, or to taste
orange slices, lemon slices, cherries and/or pineapple chunks for garnish

Fill a large pitcher with ice and add all ingredients except garnishes. Stir until sugar dissolves and taste, adjusting to personal preference. Add garnishes and serve.

GRAPEFRUIT PINEAPPLE PUNCH

2½ gallons

There always seems to be an occasion to make punch in quantity and you will impress your guests when you make fresh juice punch.

1 gallon cold water
½ cup tea leaves
46 oz. fresh grapefruit juice
46 oz. fresh pineapple juice
2 quarts ginger ale
3 cups water
6 cups sugar

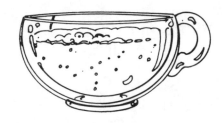

Pour cold water over the tea and let stand for 12 hours. Strain tea and mix with grapefruit juice, pineapple juice and ginger ale. Boil water and sugar together for 5 minutes and add to punch mixture. Taste and adjust sweetness to personal preference.

APPETIZERS AND SOUPS

NOTE: See *Sauces and Glazes,* page 37, for guacamole and salsa recipes, also served as appetizers.

CREAMY PINEAPPLE SPREAD

3 cups

Use this as an appetizer spread to serve with crackers, or spread it on tea breads. Consider using other fruit pulps for a change.

2 pkg. (8 oz. each) softened cream cheese
1 cup pineapple pulp, without peeling
½-1 cup flaked coconut
2 tbs. grated orange zest
¼ cup rum, optional

Mix all ingredients together in a food processor or blender and chill.

CREAMY VEGETABLE SPREAD

3 cups

This is a great way to use your vegetable pulps and to create a totally different taste sensation each time, depending on the pulp you use.

½ cup red pepper pulp, without seeds
2 green onions, sliced
2 pkg. (8 oz. each) softened cream cheese
1 cup pineapple pulp, without peeling
1 tsp. seasoning salt, or herbs of your preference
1 cup toasted, chopped pecans

Mix red pepper pulp, onions, cream cheese, pineapple pulp and seasoning together in a food processor or blender. Form into a ball or place in a pretty bowl and cover with chopped, toasted pecans. Serve chilled with crackers.

CREAM CHEESE GINGER BALL

Servings: 12

This delicious appetizer is simple; the juice can be changed for variety.

2 pkg. (8 oz. each) cream cheese
3 oz. crystallized ginger
1/4 cup fresh orange juice
1 cup toasted chopped almonds

In a food processor or blender, process crystallized ginger until it is in small pieces. Add cream cheese and orange juice. Taste and adjust the quantity of ginger to your personal preference. Chill until mixture is firm enough to form into a ball. Roll in chopped toasted almonds. Serve with crackers.

LEMON PRAWN SOUP

I've adapted this favorite Thai soup by using fresh lemon, lime and ginger root juices. Be sure to adjust these citrus juices to your personal taste. Fish sauce is available where Oriental groceries are sold.

8 large prawns, uncooked
3 cups chicken stock
4-6 hot chiles, finely chopped
1 tbs. fresh ginger root juice
¼ cup fresh lemon juice, or to taste
2 tbs. chopped cilantro
¼ cup fresh lime juice
3 tbs. fish sauce
½ lb. mushrooms (I prefer straw variety)

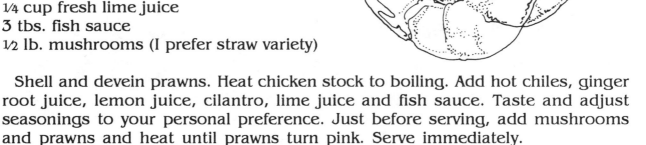

Shell and devein prawns. Heat chicken stock to boiling. Add hot chiles, ginger root juice, lemon juice, cilantro, lime juice and fish sauce. Taste and adjust seasonings to your personal preference. Just before serving, add mushrooms and prawns and heat until prawns turn pink. Serve immediately.

LEMON CHICKEN SOUP

Servings: 4

This is a great change from the standard American chicken vegetable soup. Depending on my guests, I may either increase the chiles or leave them out entirely. Again, look for fish sauce where Oriental groceries are sold.

3 cups chicken stock
1 tsp. pepper or 4 hot chiles, finely chopped
1 lb. boneless chicken meat, diced
¼ cup fresh lemon juice
3 tbs. lime juice
3 tbs. fish sauce
½ cup chopped bok choy
½ cup mushrooms (I prefer straw variety)
½-1 tsp. sugar
8 cherry tomatoes

Heat chicken stock to boiling. Add all ingredients except tomatoes. Cook slowly, uncovered, for about 10 minutes. Taste and adjust seasonings to personal preference. Add tomatoes and cook an additional 5 minutes. Serve hot.

CLAM CHOWDER

This is a good way to use potato juice which is loaded with nutrients. Potatoes, with their skins, are good for kidney ailments. They are a natural thickening agent.

⅓ lb. bacon
4 stalks of celery, chopped
1 onion, chopped
2 bunches green onions, chopped
6 garlic cloves, minced
½ cup butter
1 cup flour
1 can (20 oz.) clam juice

1¼ cups fresh potato juice
3¾ cups water
4 large potatoes, parboiled
2½ tsp. salt
1 tsp. pepper
1 tsp. thyme
½ cup half and half, or more
20 oz. chopped clams

Cut bacon into small pieces and fry in a skillet until crumbly. Remove bacon from skillet and add celery, onion, green onion and garlic. Stir for several minutes and set aside. Melt butter in a large kettle or Dutch oven and add flour, stirring constantly for several minutes to brown the roux. To roux, add clam juice, potato juice and water and stir until mixture thickens. Add salt, pepper, thyme and bacon-vegetable mixture. Add half and half and chopped clams just before serving. Taste and adjust seasonings to personal preference.
NOTE: Add additional half and half for creaminess or to slightly thin the soup.

CREAMY PLUM SOUP

Servings: 4

This makes a delightful and colorful starter course that you can garnish with a dollop of sour cream.

2 cups of plum juice with plum pulp
1 cup water
2/3 cup sugar, or to taste
1/4 tsp. cinnamon
1/8 tsp. nutmeg
pinch of salt
1/4 tsp. white pepper

1/2 cup dry white wine
1 tbs. cornstarch
1/2 cup cream
2 tbs. fresh lemon juice
1/2 cup sour cream
3 tbs. brandy, optional
sour cream for garnish, optional

Put plum juice and pulp in a large saucepan. Add water, sugar, cinnamon, nutmeg, salt and pepper. Bring to a low boil and simmer for 5 minutes. Combine wine with cornstarch and pour into soup. Stir until soup is thickened. Add cream and lemon juice. Remove from heat. Remove a little of the hot soup, mix with sour cream and return to hot soup, stirring until well mixed. Add brandy if desired and mix well. Taste soup and adjust seasonings to personal preference. Chill soup before serving. Serve with a dollop of sour cream if desired.

PARSNIP SOUP

1½ quarts

Parsnips have a natural sweet flavor and are good for people with milk intolerance. This recipe utilizes three different pulps.

1 lb. parsnips
¾ cup onion pulp
½ cup celery pulp
4 cups chicken broth
¼-½ cup spinach pulp
3 tbs. Dijon mustard
1 cup cream
salt and pepper to taste

Peel parsnips and chop into small pieces. Cook parsnips, onion pulp, celery pulp and chicken broth together until parsnips are very tender, about 15 minutes. Remove from heat and add spinach pulp, Dijon mustard, cream, salt and pepper. Taste and adjust seasonings to personal preference.

COURT BOUILLON

I use court bouillon to cook my fish, salmon, prawns and other seafood instead of plain water, so that it has a lot more flavor. This is a great way to use several pulps.

¾ cup celery pulp
½ cup carrot pulp
¼-½ cup onion pulp
1 cup white wine
½ cup chopped parsley

1 tsp. thyme
1 bay leaf
1 tbs. salt
8 whole peppercorns
3 quarts cold water

Bring all ingredients to a boil; reduce heat and simmer for 30 minutes. Bouillon will keep in an airtight container in the refrigerator for 3 days.

To use, add fish and cook approximately 10 minutes for every inch of thickness (measured at the thickest part of the fish). At this point you may remove court bouillon from the stove and actually cool fish in bouillon for extra flavor. This adds a lot of flavor to the fish, as well as moisture.

FRUIT SOUP

Servings: 4

I really enjoy fruit soups as a starter course especially during the summer months, but this one can be made year around because grapes and apples are usually available during the whole year. I like to float fruit in the soup, such as sliced nectarines or peaches because they add additional color and taste.

2 cups fresh grape juice (I prefer mixing
   grape varieties)
1 cup fresh apple juice (I prefer tart variety)
½ cup coconut cream
1-inch slice ginger root, juiced, or more to taste
½ tsp. cinnamon

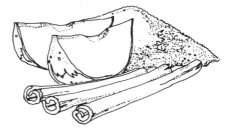

Mix all ingredients together and taste, adjusting to your personal preference.

NOTE: You may thicken this mixture by adding a little cornstarch which has been mixed with cold water and heating it.

VEGETABLE SOUP

Here is a very good way to use up excessive tomato produce, and this soup is low in calories, too.

3 quarts fresh tomato juice
1 head cabbage, sliced
1 onion, sliced
1 green bell pepper, cored and
  seeded, sliced
3-4 stalks celery, sliced

2 cups sliced carrots
6 chicken bouillon cubes
pepper to taste
pinch of cloves
a little sugar, optional, if tomatoes
  have a tendency toward bitterness

Bring tomato juice to boil in a large soup kettle and add cabbage. Add onion, green pepper, celery and carrots. Add bouillon cubes, pepper and cloves. Stir; taste and adjust to your personal preference. At this point you may want to add a little sugar if the tomatoes are on the bitter side. Simmer soup until vegetables are tender. Taste and correct seasonings again.

SAUCES, GLAZES AND JELLIES

ORANGE GLAZE/MARINADE

2 cups

This makes a marvelous glaze or marinade for any poultry or pork dish.

1 cup fresh orange juice
½ cup honey
¼ cup soy sauce
3 large garlic cloves, pressed
1 tbs. fresh ginger root juice
2 tsp. sesame oil (I prefer toasted variety)

Mix all ingredients together in a bowl. Cover meat with marinade and refrigerate for 24 hours. Or simply brush this glaze on your chicken or game hens and either bake or broil.

BARBECUE SAUCE

3 cups

Sauces are a wonderful way to use up vegetable pulp — barbecue sauce is one of the best ways.

1/4 cup onion pulp
2 tbs. butter
2 tbs. vinegar
3 tsp. Worcestershire sauce
1/2 tsp. prepared mustard
2 tsp. brown sugar
4 tsp. fresh lemon juice
1 bottle (14 oz.) ketchup
1/2 cup water
1/4 cup celery pulp
salt to taste

Brown onion pulp in butter. Add remaining ingredients and simmer until slightly thickened. Because pulp is somewhat stringy, you may want to strain this sauce.

SATEH SAUCE

Thai food has become very popular, and especially sateh sauce. This is normally served on marinated chicken or pork skewers.

¼ cup vegetable oil
2 garlic cloves, minced
¼ cup onion pulp
½ tsp. ground chili pepper
2 tsp. fresh lime juice
½ tsp. curry powder
¼ cup fresh lemon juice

1 cup coconut milk
½ cup milk
¼ tsp. cinnamon
3 bay leaves
2 tbs. fish sauce
3 tbs. dark brown sugar
1 cup chunky peanut butter

Heat oil in a skillet. Add garlic, onion pulp, chili pepper, lime juice, curry powder and lemon juice. Cook for 2 minutes. Stir in remaining ingredients, reduce heat and simmer until sauce thickens, about 30 minutes.

MANGO SAUCE

3 cups

I especially love this on chicken or any poultry dish, and because there is no cooking it is incredibly simple.

2 cups mango pulp
1 cup papaya pulp
½-1 jalapeño pepper, finely chopped
2 tsp. soy sauce
1 tbs. fresh lemon juice
2 tsp. chopped chives

Combine all ingredients together. Taste and adjust to your personal preference. Serve over cooked poultry dishes.

LIME BUTTER SAUCE

If you're always looking for something interesting to do with vegetables, this may become one of your favorites. I particularly like this on something colorful like a combination of sugar snaps, peas and carrots.

½ cup butter
¼ cup fresh lime juice
2 tsp. fresh ginger root juice
1 tbs. sugar, or to taste
salt and pepper to taste

Melt butter in a skillet. Add lime juice, ginger root juice, sugar, salt and pepper. Add steamed vegetables and toss until heated through. Serve immediately.

KAANIPALI SAUCE

3 cups

This a wonderful tropical sauce that I've adapted to use pulps. It is wonderful served over any poultry or pork dish.

2 tsp. butter
1/4 cup onion pulp
2 garlic cloves, crushed
1 cup apple pulp, without seeds
  or stems
1 cup tomato pulp
2 tsp. flour
1/2 tsp. thyme

1/4-1/2 tsp. cinnamon
1 tbs. curry powder
1 tbs. sugar, or to taste
2 tsp. salt
1 1/2 cups chicken broth
1/2 cup cream
1/3 cup white wine

Melt butter in a saucepan. Sauté onion pulp, garlic, apple pulp and tomato pulp for 2 minutes. Remove garlic. Reduce heat to low, stir in flour and cook for 2 minutes. Add thyme, cinnamon, curry powder, sugar, salt, broth, cream and wine. Simmer 5 minutes.

NOTE: If sauce appears to be too thick when sautéing the pulps together, add either vegetable juices, water or additional chicken stock to thin.

PINEAPPLE SALSA

3 cups

This unusual tropical salsa is a sauce that I use on fish dishes, especially salmon.

2 cups pineapple pulp, without peelings
¼ cup red bell pepper pulp
¼ cup green bell pepper pulp
¼ cup finely minced red onion
¼ cup finely chopped cilantro
1 tbs. fresh lime juice
1-2 tsp. minced jalapeño chiles, or to taste
salt to taste

Combine all ingredients in a small bowl. Season to taste. This can be prepared several hours in advance of use. Cover and refrigerate.

AVOCADO SALSA

Lime is a delightful addition to avocado dishes as an alternative to lemon because it gives it a slightly more exotic flavor.

4 large ripe avocados
3-4 tbs. fresh lime juice, with peeling
1 tsp. sugar, or to taste
¼ cup chopped red onion
1 tbs. chopped cilantro, or to taste
¼ tsp. red pepper flakes
1 small tomato, diced

Peel, pit and dice avocados and place in a bowl. Add remaining ingredients and mix. Taste and adjust seasoning to your personal preference.

PEACH SAUCE

This makes a marvelous sauce that is especially good with spareribs.

2 cups peach pulp
⅔ cup ketchup
⅔ cup vinegar
¼ cup soy sauce
1 cup brown sugar
2 garlic cloves, minced
2 tsp. fresh ginger root juice
salt and pepper to taste

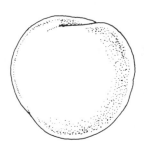

Mix all ingredients together in a food processor or blender. Taste and adjust seasoning to your personal preference. Pour this sauce over meat that you are roasting in the oven, basting several times with sauce during the cooking process.

SWEET AND SOUR SAUCE

1½ cups

This is another wonderful sweet and sour sauce that I particularly like to serve over chicken or with appetizers like rumaki.

3 tbs. dark brown sugar
3 tbs. vinegar, or fresh lemon juice
3 tbs. ketchup
1 tbs. soy sauce
1 cup fresh pineapple juice
3 tbs. cornstarch

Mix all ingredients together and pour into a saucepan. Heat and stir until thickened.

GUACAMOLE SAUCE

1½ cups

This is a favorite guacamole recipe that I've adapted to use pulps and fresh juices. Cilantro is an herb that is indispensable in Mexican cookery and tastes something like hot mint.

1-2 garlic cloves
2 tbs. onion pulp
4 ripe avocados, peeled, seeded, cut
  into chunks
salt to taste
2-4 drops Tabasco

3 tbs. fresh lemon juice
1 chile, optional
1 tomato, seeded and chopped
1 avocado, peeled, seeded and
  chopped
2 tsp. chopped cilantro, or to taste

Using the steel blade of a food processor or blender, mince garlic. Add onion and avocado chunks. Process until smooth. Add seasonings and adjust to your personal taste. Chiles are optional and range from mild to very hot — add sparingly so that you don't cover up the true avocado flavor. Just before serving, add chopped tomato, avocado and cilantro and mix with a spoon so that you have some texture in your guacamole.

SAUCE CHORON

2 cups

This is a favorite of my sister-in-law Christie. She likes to serve it on poached fish, vegetables or even on top of poached eggs.

3 minced shallots, or 1 tbs. onion pulp
4 tbs. white wine
¾ cup melted butter
4 egg yolks
⅓-½ cup fresh orange juice
1 tbs. orange zest
1 tbs. tomato paste
salt and white pepper to taste

Place minced shallots and white wine in a small saucepan and cook until mixture is reduced (shallots should be soft and wine mostly evaporated). Melt butter until bubbling. Combine egg yolks, orange juice and zest, tomato paste, salt and pepper in the bowl of a food processor and start machine running. Slowly begin to drop shallot and butter mixture through the feed tube to create a thick sauce. Taste and correct seasoning to your personal preference.

WILD GAME SAUCE

3 cups

Occasionally I am given some hunter's prize, and this is one of my favorite sauces to serve over duck, pheasant or any poultry dish.

2 tbs. onion pulp
¼ cup butter
1 lb. plums, juice and pulp included
1 tsp. fresh ginger root juice
2 tbs. chili sauce
¼ cup fresh lemon juice
2 tbs. soy sauce
¼ cup brown sugar
¼ cup sour cream

Sauté onion pulp in butter for a few minutes. Add remaining ingredients except sour cream and cook for about 15 minutes. Remove and process in a blender or food processor until smooth. Add sour cream and process again. Taste and adjust seasonings.

HONEY CURRY GLAZE

2 cups

This is particularly good on duck, pork, or any poultry dish.

1 cup honey
½ cup fresh lemon juice
½ cup fresh orange juice
3 tbs. curry, or to taste

Mix all ingredients together. Baste the glaze on meat before roasting. Baste several times during the roasting process.

TROPICAL POULTRY SAUCE

2 cups

An extraordinary combination of fruits makes this sauce unique and delectable. It goes especially well with duck or any poultry dish.

¼ cup butter
3 firm bananas
1 can (11 oz.) lichee nuts, drained
½ cup orange marmalade
1½ cups fresh orange juice
½ cup orange liqueur (Grand Marnier, orange curacao or triple sec)

Melt butter in a saucepan. Add sliced bananas and sauté in butter for a few minutes. Add remaining ingredients except liqueur and stir together. Heat liqueur (optional), ignite and add to sauce. Serve over cooked meat.

APPLE MINT SAUCE

2½ cups

This sauce is good with lamb dishes and also goes well with pork.

2 Golden Delicious apples
1 tbs. fresh lemon juice
2 tbs. butter
½ cup apple mint jelly
2 tsp. chopped fresh mint leaves, or ½ tsp. dry mint
1¾ cups fresh apple juice
3 tbs. cornstarch mixed with 3 tbs. water
2 tbs. apple brandy, or to taste, optional

Peel apples, cut into slices, and toss with lemon juice. Sauté apple slices in butter until tender, about 2 minutes. Stir in apple mint jelly, apple juice and cornstarch mixture. Bring to a boil, stirring constantly. When mixture thickens, remove from heat and serve alongside your lamb dish. At this point, you may want to add some apple brandy: heat brandy, ignite and pour on the sauce just before serving.
NOTE: You may want to add a few drops of green food coloring for eye appeal.

PINEAPPLE CHUTNEY

2½ cups

For those people who love pineapple juice (especially those with arthritis or stomach problems), this is a great way to use up the pineapple pulp.

2 cups pineapple pulp, without peelings
1 cup finely chopped dried apricots
1 cup chopped red onion
½ cup chopped red bell pepper
½ cup light corn syrup
2-3 oz. crystallized ginger, diced into small pieces

5 tbs. vinegar
¼ cup sugar
2 tsp. allspice
½ tsp. dry mustard
½ tsp. red pepper flakes
¼ tsp. salt, or to taste)
¼ tsp. cloves

Combine all ingredients in a heavy saucepan and bring to a boil. Reduce heat and simmer until mixture begins to thicken, stirring occasionally, about 20 minutes. Taste and adjust seasonings to personal preference. Cool.

CRANBERRY PINEAPPLE CHUTNEY

6 cups

A great holiday chutney that can serve as either an appetizer or alongside poultry or possibly even a pork dinner.

4 cups fresh cranberries
1 cup pineapple pulp
1¼ cups water
1 cup raisins
2 cups sugar, or to taste
½ tsp. ginger
½ tsp. cinnamon
¼ tsp. allspice
¼ tsp. salt

Combine all ingredients in a saucepan and cook over medium heat until cranberries burst and mixture is thick. Cool and refrigerate.

RHUBARB SYRUP

2 cups

Rhubarb is not the easiest thing to juice but it is very flavorful. I like to use this sauce on top of pancakes or desserts such as bread pudding.

1 cup fresh rhubarb juice
1/2 cup light corn syrup
1/2 cup sugar, or to taste
1 1/2 tbs. cornstarch
2 tbs. water

In a heavy saucepan, heat rhubarb juice, corn syrup and sugar, stirring well. Mix cornstarch and water together and add to heated rhubarb mixture. Stir until thickened.

LIME SAUCE

Consider using this sauce to serve over fresh fruit, on top of desserts or even in tart shells.

1 cup water
¾ cup sugar
½ cup fresh lime juice
dash salt
3 tbs. cornstarch
food coloring, optional

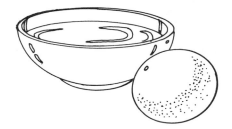

Mix all ingredients together in a saucepan, heat and stir until thickened.

RASPBERRY SAUCE

1½ cups

Raspberry sauce can be used to top so many things, such as ice cream, all types of desserts including chocolate desserts, and breakfast items such as French toast, waffles or pancakes.

1 cup fresh raspberry juice
⅓ cup fresh orange juice
½ cup sugar, or more to taste
2 tbs. cornstarch
2 tbs. seedless raspberry jam

Pour raspberry juice and orange juice into a saucepan and mix in sugar. Remove a small amount of juice and mix with cornstarch until smooth; return to saucepan and stir. Bring to a boil, stirring constantly until mixture thickens. Add seedless raspberry jam, mix well, cover and refrigerate until sauce is well chilled.

BLUEBERRY SAUCE

2½ cups

I like to use this sauce on French toast, ice cream, or on top of dessert mousses.

1 cup sugar
1½ tbs. cornstarch
dash of salt
pinch of nutmeg
1 cup water
1 cup fresh blueberry juice

In a saucepan, mix sugar, cornstarch, salt and nutmeg. Stir in water and blueberry juice and cook over medium heat until thick. Taste and adjust sugar or spices to your personal preference.

LEMON CUSTARD GLAZE

1½ cups

This is a great glaze to use on cheesecakes, lemon cake, or to use as a sauce.

2 eggs
4 egg yolks
¾ cup sugar
½ cup fresh lemon juice
1 tbs. grated lemon zest
½ cup butter

Combine eggs, egg yolks, sugar, lemon juice and lemon zest together in a heavy saucepan. Whisk over medium heat until mixture thickens. Do not boil or mixture will curdle. Remove from heat and stir in butter. Spread on the dessert while custard is still warm.

ORANGE CARAMEL SAUCE

2 cups

This sauce is delicious served over ice cream or frozen yogurt.

2 cups brown sugar
1½ cups fresh orange juice
6 tbs. butter

Using a heavy bottom saucepan, mix ingredients together and stir over medium heat until sugar dissolves. Increase heat and boil gently until mixture is reduced to approximately 2 cups, about 15 minutes.

LIME JELLY

4 cups

When limes are in season and plentiful, I like to make lime jelly, which is great with breakfast or served over cream cheese as an appetizer.

2 cups fresh lime juice, with peel
1 cup sugar

Place lime juice and sugar into a heavy saucepan and heat until sugar dissolves. Simmer, stirring constantly, until 220° on a candy thermometer is reached. Pour into hot sterilized jars and seal.

APPLE JELLY

Apple jelly is a favorite at our house and when apple season comes I like to make loads. This again is great with toast, but also consider serving it over cream cheese as an appetizer.

2 cups fresh apple juice
2 tbs. fresh lemon juice
2 cups sugar, or more to taste
1/4 cup whole mint leaves

Place apple juice, lemon juice and sugar in a saucepan and heat until sugar dissolves. Simmer, stirring constantly, until 220° on a candy thermometer is reached. Remove from heat and add mint leaves. Pour into hot sterilized jars and seal.

NOTE: Using the apple juice this way is going to produce a darker jelly than the clear apple jelly that you are used to in the stores.

ZUCCHINI JELLY

6 cups

For that time of year when zucchini is abundant, here is an unusual way to use it, and it tastes great. I use this for breakfast jelly and also on top of cream cheese, served with crackers for an appetizer.

6 cups of zucchini, unpeeled and shredded (you may use zucchini pulp)
3 cups sugar
½ cup fresh lemon juice
1 cup pineapple pulp, without peeling
1 pkg. (6 oz.) apricot gelatin

Combine zucchini and sugar in a large saucepan. Bring to a boil over medium high heat while stirring. Cook for 6 minutes and then add lemon juice and pineapple pulp. Bring to a boil and cook for 1 minute, stirring constantly. Remove from heat and stir in apricot gelatin until dissolved. Pour into sterilized jars and seal with paraffin.

NOTE: I have tried it with zucchini pulp as opposed to shredded zucchini and warn you that it will not look as appetizing.

SALADS AND DRESSINGS

MOLDED LIME SALAD

This is an easy family favorite that can be served any time of year.

1 pkg. (6 oz.) lime gelatin
1 cup boiling water
1 cup mayonnaise
1 can evaporated milk
1 cup shredded sharp cheddar cheese
1½ cups pineapple pulp, without peelings
½-1 cup chopped toasted walnuts

Dissolve gelatin in boiling water; cool until partially set. Beat cooled gelatin with an electric beater. Add mayonnaise and evaporated milk, beating well. Add shredded cheese and pineapple pulp and finish with toasted chopped walnuts. Chill for several hours before serving.

PINEAPPLE CHEESE MOLDED SALAD

This is a wonderful way to use your pineapple pulp. Please remember to always use pulp which does not contain peelings in cooking.

1 pkg. unflavored gelatin
2/3 cup cold water
1/2 cup fresh pineapple juice
1/2 cup sugar
3 tbs. fresh lemon juice
1 jar (5 oz.) pimiento cheese spread

1 cup pineapple pulp,
  without peelings
1 can (11 oz.) mandarin oranges
1/2 cup chopped nuts
1 cup cream, whipped

Add gelatin to cold water and let soak for about 5 minutes. In a saucepan, simmer pineapple juice and sugar for 5 minutes. Add lemon juice and gelatin water and stir until thoroughly dissolved. Blend in cheese spread and beat until smooth. Chill until partially set. Stir in pineapple pulp, mandarin oranges and nuts. Fold in whipped cream and pour into a 1½-quart mold. Chill until firm.

CRANBERRY MOLDED SALAD

Servings: 6

Molded salads are a good way to use up fruit pulps. This salad utilizes both cranberry juice and pineapple pulp in the same recipe.

1 cup fresh cranberry juice
½ cup sugar, or to taste
1 pkg. (3 oz.) raspberry gelatin
2 oranges, peeled and chopped
½ cup pineapple pulp, without peelings
¾ cup sour cream
¼ cup chopped nuts

Heat fresh cranberry juice with sugar to boiling point. Taste and adjust sweetness to your personal preference. Remove from heat and stir in gelatin until dissolved. Chill mixture until partially set. Fold in orange pieces and any juice saved from chopping oranges. Fold in pineapple pulp, sour cream and chopped nuts. Pour into a 1-quart mold. Chill until firm.

ORANGE SHERBET SALAD

Servings: 12

I love this salad because it seems to go with any meal at any time of the year. You can't to wrong when you mix orange and pineapple together.

1 pkg. (6 oz.) orange gelatin
2 cups boiling water
1 pint orange sherbet
1-2 cans mandarin oranges
1½ cups pineapple pulp, without peelings
2-3 bananas, sliced
1 cup cream, whipped

Mix gelatin with hot water and add sherbet. Chill until partially set. Fold in oranges, pineapple pulp, bananas and whipped cream. Pour into a 9x13-inch pan or favorite mold and chill until completely set.

MOLDED FRUIT SALAD

Servings: 12

Don't limit yourself to the pulps used in this recipe. Be creative and change the flavor of the gelatin to give variety to your salads.

1 pkg. (6 oz.) strawberry gelatin
2 cups boiling water
1⅓ cups fruit juice (orange, pineapple, or even cranberry)
1 cup cranberry pulp
sugar to taste
½ cup orange pulp
1 cup apple pulp, without seeds or stems
2 mashed bananas
1 cup pineapple pulp, without peelings

Mix gelatin with boiling water and fruit juices and cool until partially set. Mix cranberry pulp with sugar in a saucepan (adding a little cranberry juice or water if pulp is too dry). Stir until sugar dissolves, tasting and adjusting sweetness to your personal taste. Mix remaining ingredients with partially set gelatin. Pour into a mold and chill until completely set.

APPLE CABBAGE SLAW

Servings: 6

I think apple makes cole slaw special, and by using the carrot pulp as an alternative to shredded carrot you're putting to good use both pulp and juices in this recipe.

3 cups shredded green cabbage, or red, or combination
½ cup carrot pulp, or shredded carrot
1 coarsely chopped red apple
½ cup diced green bell pepper
¼ diced red onion
¼ cup fresh lemon juice, with peel
3 tbs. sugar, or to taste
2 tbs. vegetable oil
½ tsp. minced garlic
¼ tsp. celery seed

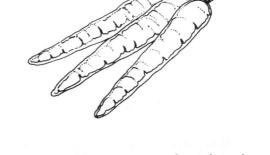

Combine cabbage, carrot pulp, apple, green pepper and red onion. Blend together remaining dressing ingredients and toss over vegetables. Taste and adjust seasonings to your personal preference. Refrigerate until chilled.

CITRUS AND AVOCADO SALAD

Servings: 4

This makes a great starter course for a meal. You can substitute grapefruit segments and grapefruit juice for the orange segments and orange juice for a totally different flavor.

1 cup vegetable oil (I like to blend several types of oil)
¼ cup balsamic vinegar
½ cup fresh orange juice, or grapefruit juice
¼ cup fresh lemon juice
¼ cup sugar, or to taste
½ tsp. salt
½ tsp. dry mustard

½ tbs. onion pulp
2-3 oranges, peeled and segmented, or grapefruit
2 avocados, peeled and sliced
1 cup pecans
2 tbs. butter
lettuce or spinach, or combination of greens

Combine oil, vinegar, orange juice, lemon juice, sugar, salt, dry mustard and onion pulp in a food processor or blender and blend well. Marinate orange segments or grapefruit segments and avocado in dressing for 2 hours before serving. Sauté pecans in butter until toasted. Tear salad greens into bite-size pieces and toss with marinated oranges and avocados. Sprinkle pecans over top and serve.

AVOCADO SALAD

This is a simple salad that can be made quite elegant with the addition of a little caviar.

2 heads butter lettuce
4 avocados (I prefer the Haas variety)
¼ cup fresh lemon juice
1 cup sour cream
red and black caviar for garnish

Wash and coarsely tear butter lettuce and arrange on salad plates. Fan avocado slices on top of lettuce. Mix sour cream with lemon juice and drizzle over avocados. Garnish with one very small spoonful each of red and black caviar side by side.

PAPAYA SALAD

Servings: 6

When I begin to feel the need to run away to a nice tropical vacation and can't, I sometimes fix exotic foods to make me feel better. This is one of them. Cut the avocado last to prevent discoloration.

½ cup sugar
2 tsp. salt
½ tsp. dry mustard
½ cup white vinegar
½ cup vegetable oil
1 tbs. onion pulp

¼ cup papaya pulp, without peel
   but including seeds
2 heads lettuce (butter, romaine,
   Bibb, or combination)
1 papaya, seeded and sliced
1 avocado, seeded and sliced
6-8 water chestnuts, sliced

Make dressing by combining sugar, salt, dry mustard, white vinegar, oil, onion pulp and papaya pulp. Process until smooth in a food processor or blender. Tear lettuce into bite-size pieces, wash and dry. Place lettuce on individual salad plates. Place papaya and avocado slices alternately around plates. Sprinkle with sliced water chestnuts and drizzle with papaya dressing.

NOTE: The papaya seeds have a peppery flavor and they actually impart a unique flavor to the dressing. You may want to increase the pulp for a more potent flavor.

LIME CHUTNEY CHICKEN SALAD

Lime gives this salad a zesty fresh taste.

1 cup mayonnaise
½ cup chutney
1 tsp. curry powder
1 tbs. grated lime zest
¼ cup fresh lime juice, with peel
½ tsp. salt, or to taste
4 cups diced cooked white chicken meat
1½ cups fresh pineapple, cut into chunks
½ cup sliced green onions
½ cup toasted slivered almonds

Combine mayonnaise, chutney, curry powder, lime zest, lime juice and salt together in a bowl. Add chicken, pineapple and green onion and toss. Taste and adjust seasonings to personal preference. Just before serving, add slivered almonds.

BEAN SALAD

Servings: 12

Bean salad tastes best with a sweet-and-sour type of dressing. Make this salad with an assortment of colors to give it real eye appeal.

1 lb. dried beans (combination of types)
1 cup olive oil
½ cup fresh lemon juice
¼ cup red wine vinegar (I prefer balsamic)
1½ cups finely chopped celery
¼ cup finely chopped red bell pepper

¼ cup finely chopped green bell pepper
3 tbs. finely chopped parsley
2 tbs. chopped red onion
2 tsp. salt
½ tsp. thyme
¼ cup sugar

Soak beans overnight and then throw out the soaking water. Cook beans in fresh water until tender, following package directions. I like to use several types of beans in my bean salad, so I test the largest bean for tenderness. Drain beans and rinse in cold water. Mix remaining ingredients together and pour over beans. Cover and marinate at least 4 hours.

CELERY SEED DRESSING

I use this on fruit salads or tossed salads that have fruit in them.

1 cup vegetable oil
⅔ cup sugar
3 tbs. vinegar
2 tbs. fresh lemon juice
2 tbs. onion pulp
1 tsp. Dijon mustard
1 tsp. celery seed
dash of salt and pepper

Using a food processor or blender, process all ingredients until smooth. Taste and adjust to personal preference. Cover and refrigerate.

PINEAPPLE FRUIT DRESSING

3 cups

I am always trying to find alternative ways to dress up fruit salad and this is another favorite.

1 cup sugar
1½ tbs. cornstarch
2 eggs
1 cup fresh pineapple juice
1 cup cream
few drops food coloring, optional

Mix together sugar and cornstarch. In a saucepan, beat eggs lightly and add pineapple juice. Mix in sugar and cornstarch and stir until mixture comes to a low boil and thickens. Cool and then refrigerate. Whip cream and fold it into cooled mixture. At this point you may add a few drops of yellow food coloring to give it a richer appearance. Serve over fruit salad.

ORANGE DRESSING

1½ cups

Orange dressing goes so well on spinach salad and also on any green salad that has some fruit in it.

½ lb. sliced bacon
¾ cup fresh orange juice
1 tbs. onion pulp
¼ cup olive oil, or blend of oils
¼ cup balsamic vinegar

Cut bacon into small pieces and fry until crisp. Remove bacon from pan and drain on paper towels. Pour off drippings, reserving ¼ cup. Fry onion pulp in bacon drippings for a few minutes. Combine orange juice, onion pulp, olive oil and vinegar in a blender or food processor and process until smooth. Mix fried bacon bits in with dressing and serve over salads.

FRENCH VINIAGRETTE DRESSING

1½ cups

This is a classic viniagrette dressing that I use as a marinade, or as a dressing for salads or vegetables.

1 cup olive oil
3 tbs. fresh lemon juice, with peel
3 tbs. balsamic vinegar
2 tbs. Dijon mustard
1 garlic clove, minced
1 tsp. basil
1 tsp. oregano
½ tsp. tarragon
salt and pepper to taste

Combine all ingredients in a food processor or a blender. Adjust seasonings to your personal taste.

PESTO SALAD DRESSING

2½ cups

Pesto dressing is a favorite, especially on pasta salads. I particularly like it on linguini that has been mixed with vegetables and shrimp.

2 eggs
1 cup olive oil

¼ cup fresh lemon juice, with peel
½-1 cup bottled pesto

In a food processor or blender, process eggs for about ½ minute. Slowly add oil in a thin stream. When mixture thickens, add lemon juice and blend. Then add pesto and blend. Taste and add more lemon juice or pesto to your personal preference. Chill and serve over pasta salads.

TART AND TANGY DRESSING

2 cups

I like to serve this on any type of tossed vegetable salads, especially salads with green or red bell peppers.

⅔ cup vinegar (I prefer balsamic)
⅔ cup fresh lemon juice
½ cup olive oil
2 garlic cloves, minced

2 tsp. salt
1 tsp. dill seed
1 tsp. tarragon
¼ tsp. pepper

Process all ingredients in a food processor or a blender until smooth.

COLD AND FRUITY DESSERTS

CRANBERRY PEAR SORBET

Servings: 8

A wonderful holiday palate refresher that I like to either start a meal with or possibly use as a simple ending to a heavy meal.

1⅓ cups sugar
1⅓ cups water
1 cup cranberry juice mixed with the pulp
2 cups pear juice
1⅓ cups orange juice
3-4 tbs. Pear William, or pear brandy
2 tbs. fresh lemon juice
½ tsp. ginger

Combine sugar and water in a saucepan and heat until sugar is dissolved without stirring. Remove from heat before syrup boils, and chill. Mix chilled sugar syrup with cranberry juice, pear juice, Pear William and lemon juice. Pour into a metal pan and freeze. Cut frozen sorbet into pieces and process either in a food processor or blender until smooth and fluffy. Refreeze and serve later.

ORANGE SORBET

Servings: 8

This is an unusual sorbet that I like to serve at brunches because of the citrus juices mixed with the vodka.

¾ cup sugar
¾ cup water
1 cup fresh orange juice
¼ cup fresh lemon juice
1 tsp. orange extract
2 tbs. vodka

Mix sugar in water in a saucepan and heat until sugar is dissolved without stirring. Remove from heat just before the syrup boils, and chill. Add sugar syrup to remaining ingredients and pour into a metal pan. Freeze until solid, cut into pieces, and beat with either a food processor or a blender until mixture is smooth and fluffy. Refreeze and serve.

PEAR SORBET

Servings: 8

Pears are wonderful for their calming properties and this is a great way to use up the pear pulp.

2 cups pear pulp, without seeds or stems
¾ cup fresh pineapple juice
1 cup sugar
½ tsp. salt
1 pkg. (3 oz.) cream cheese, softened
½ cup cream
2 tbs. fresh lemon juice
2-4 tbs. Pear William, or any pear liqueur

Mix pear pulp with pineapple juice and process until smooth in a food processor or blender. Add remaining ingredients and adjust either sugar or liqueurs to your personal preference. Pour into a container and freeze until solid. Remove from freezer, cut into chunks, and blend until smooth with either a food processor or a blender. Refreeze and serve.

GINGER PEAR SORBET

Servings: 8

This is a light and refreshing frozen dessert or palate refresher. The crystallized ginger is an unusual addition that can be increased or decreased to your personal preference, but it really gives this dish an unusual appeal.

2 oz. crystallized ginger
2 cups fresh pear juice
2 cups water
½ cup sugar, or to taste
⅓ cup fresh lemon juice
1 tbs. grated lemon zest

Using a blender or food processor, process crystallized ginger until it is broken into small pieces. Then, combine remaining ingredients and blend until smooth. Taste and adjust to your personal preference by adding additional sugar, ginger or lemon juice. Freeze until solid. Break into chunks and process again in blender or food processor. Refreeze and serve.

GRAPEFRUIT GINGER SORBET

4 cups

This is another great refreshing sorbet that I use quite often for brunches or as a palate refresher in heavy meals.

3 cups fresh grapefruit juice
¾ cup sugar, or to taste
1 tbs. fresh ginger root juice

In a saucepan, combine 1 cup of grapefruit juice, sugar and ginger root juice and boil until sugar is dissolved. Let mixture cool and then stir in 2 remaining cups of grapefruit juice. Cover and freeze until solid. Remove frozen juice mixture from freezer, cut into chunks and process in a food processor or blender until mushy. Refreeze and serve.

PINEAPPLE SORBET

Servings: 6

I like the combination of pineapple and bananas together. This makes a simple palate refresher or dessert.

2½ cups sugar
2 cups water
2 cups pineapple pulp, without peel
1 banana
½ tsp. vanilla extract

Mix sugar and water together in a small pot and bring to a boil for about 2 minutes. Remove and cool. Place pineapple pulp and banana in a food processor or blender and puree until smooth. Add 1½ cups of chilled sugar syrup. Add vanilla extract and freeze. Once frozen, cut into chunks and process again to make mixture fluffy. Refreeze and serve.

FRUITED SHERBET

Servings: 12

You can use you imagination about the types of fruits you use in this sherbet — this is only one suggestion.

5 bananas
1 cup fresh orange juice
½ cup fresh lemon juice
1 cup fresh cranberry juice
2 cups fresh apple juice
2½ cups sugar
3 egg whites

With a food processor or blender, mash bananas until smooth. Add juices and sugar; process until smooth. Pour this mixture into 9x13-inch pan and freeze until almost solid (mixture should be somewhat mushy), about 2 hours.

Beat egg whites until stiff. Beat fruit mixture with a beater at low speed. Gently fold in stiff egg whites, return to pan and refreeze until mushy again. Beat mixture again, cover, and refreeze. Serve.

LEMON SHERBET

A summer must! I like to serve sherbets for dessert in the summer because they are refreshing, light and simple.

2 egg whites
2¼ cups sugar
1 cup water
1½ cups fresh lemon juice, with peel
1 tbs. lemon zest

Beat egg whites until very stiff. Heat sugar and water in a saucepan until sugar dissolves, without stirring. Continue heating until mixture reaches full boil. Drizzle hot sugar syrup into beaten egg whites, whisking until all syrup is incorporated. Add lemon juice. Cover and freeze until solid. Remove from freezer, cut into chunks, and process with a blender or food processor until light and fluffy. Refreeze and serve.

LEMON LIME PIE

A quick and easy fruit dessert that makes people think you spent hours in the kitchen!

1 pkg. (3 oz.) lime gelatin, or lemon
1 cup boiling water
1 cup sugar
1 cup fresh lemon juice, with peel
1 cup chilled evaporated milk
1 tbs. fresh lemon juice, with peel
one 9-inch graham cracker pie crust, baked

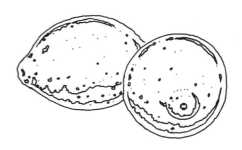

Combine lime gelatin with boiling water and stir until dissolved. Add sugar and lemon juice. Refrigerate until almost stiff. Meanwhile, mix 1 tbs. lemon juice with chilled evaporated milk and whip until stiff. Beat partially set gelatin mixture and whipped milk at low speed with an electric mixer. Pour into prebaked pie shell. Chill at least 1 hour or overnight.

CHILLED LEMON SOUFFLÉ

Servings: 8

In the summer I prefer a chilled soufflé to a cooked one. Again, this is a light dessert that's ideal after a heavy meal.

1 pkg. unflavored gelatin
1/4 cup cold water
6 egg yolks
1 cup sugar

2/3 cup fresh lemon juice, with peel
2 tbs. grated lemon zest
4 egg whites
1 1/2 cups cream

Butter and sugar a 1-quart soufflé dish. Cut a piece of parchment or waxed paper long enough to go around the dish and fold the paper in half lengthwise. Brush sides of paper with butter and sprinkle with sugar. Tie paper around the dish with buttered side turned inward and extending 2 inches above the rim. Soften gelatin in cold water. Beat egg yolks in sugar until thick and light. Add lemon juice and cook over low heat until thick, stirring constantly. Mix in softened gelatin and lemon zest until gelatin is dissolved. Remove from heat and cool. Beat egg whites until stiff but not dry. Fold egg whites into cold lemon mixture. Whip cream until soft peaks form and fold into lemon mixture. Pour into prepared soufflé dish and freeze. Serve frozen.

ELEGANT STRAWBERRIES

Servings: 6

Occasionally I like to serve a flaming dessert because it impresses people so. It's really quite simple as long as you remember to heat the liqueur separately, ignite it and then pour it over the finished dessert.

½ cup sugar
2 tbs. cornstarch
⅔ cup fresh orange juice
⅓ cup orange liqueur (Grand Marnier preferred)
1 pint fresh strawberries, washed and stemmed

Mix cornstarch and sugar together in a saucepan. Stir in orange juice. Bring mixture to a gentle boil, add strawberries and remove from heat. In a small saucepan, heat orange liqueur until very warm and ignite with a long match. Pour over orange-strawberry mixture and spoon over ice cream or frozen yogurt.

LEMON SNOW

For a really light dessert, this is perfect. It's a very old-fashioned dessert that I serve after heavy meals. Serve it with lemon sauce on top and accompanied with a crisp cookie.

⅔ cup sugar
1 envelope unflavored gelatin
1½ cups boiling water

⅓ cup fresh lemon juice, with peel
1 tsp. lemon zest
3 egg whites

Combine sugar and gelatin together and add boiling water, stirring until gelatin is dissolved. Stir in lemon juice and lemon zest. Chill mixture until it is syrupy. Beat egg whites until stiff, add syrupy mixture and beat until mixture begins to thicken slightly, about 5 minutes. Pour into a serving dish and chill 2 to 3 hours. Serve with lemon sauce drizzled over the top.

Lemon Sauce

½ cup sugar
1½ tbs. cornstarch
1 tbs. grated lemon zest

¼ cup fresh lemon juice
1 cup water

Combine sugar, cornstarch and lemon zest in a saucepan. Whisk in lemon juice and water; bring to a boil, stirring constantly until thickened.

FRESH FRUIT JUICE GELATIN

4 cups

For jello lovers this is a great treat. Use any of your favorite fresh fruit juices (except pineapple) and enjoy a healthy dessert that tastes good!

4 cups fresh juice (apple, peach, pear, orange, etc.)
2 pkg. unflavored gelatin

Mix 1 cup of juice with 2 packages of gelatin and heat on low until gelatin dissolves, approximately 3 minutes. Remove from heat and stir in remaining juice. Chill until set.

NOTE: You may also add fresh fruit to the gelatin after the gelatin has set slightly.

FROM THE BAKERY

LEMON WALNUT BREAD

2 loaves

This makes a marvelous, moist lemon bread that I like especially for afternoon tea.

1 cup butter
2 cups sugar
4 eggs
3 cups flour
½ tsp. soda

½ tsp. salt
1 cup buttermilk
1 cup chopped walnuts
2 tbs. fresh lemon juice, with peel

Preheat oven to 325°. Line 2 loaf pans with brown paper and butter paper and sides of pans. Cream together butter and sugar; beat in eggs one at a time. Mix flour with soda and salt and add alternately with buttermilk, beating well. Add chopped walnuts and 2 tbs. of fresh lemon juice. Pour into prepared pans and bake for 1 hour. While loaves are still warm, pierce tops with a fork and spoon glaze over them. Cool thoroughly before slicing.

Glaze
6 tbs. fresh lemon juice

1 cup sugar

Mix fresh lemon juice and sugar in a saucepan and cook until sugar is dissolved.

FRESH ORANGE CAKE

Servings: 12

This moist orange cake has a wonderful thick orange filling and can be glazed with either an orange icing or a chocolate glaze.

½ cup butter
½ cups sugar
2 eggs
1½ tsps. orange extract
2½ cups flour
2½ tsp. baking powder
1 tsp. salt
1½ cups milk or fresh orange juice

½ cup semi-sweet chocolate chips
1 cup sugar
6 tbs. cornstarch
dash of salt
1⅓ cups fresh orange juice
4 egg yolks, lightly beaten
4 tbs. butter
1 tsp. orange extract

Preheat oven to 350°. Line two 9-inch round cake pans with brown paper and butter paper and sides of pans. Cream butter and sugar. Add eggs and beat well. Add orange extract. Mix flour, baking powder and salt together and add alternately with milk (or orange juice) to butter mixture, beating well after each addition. Fold in chocolate chips. Pour batter into prepared bake pans and bake 30 minutes. Cool before adding the filling.

To prepare filling: Combine sugar, cornstarch, and salt in a saucepan; stir in fresh orange juice. Cook over medium heat until thick, and then stir about half the hot mixture into beaten egg yolks. Return egg yolk mixture to saucepan; cook until very thick, about 2 minutes. Remove from heat and stir in butter and orange extract. Cover surface of filling with waxed paper and chill. Spread orange filling between two layers of cake, or if desired split cake into four layers and fill between layers. Drizzle orange glaze or chocolate glaze over top.

Orange glaze:

1 cup powdered sugar
4 tbs. softened butter

4 oz. cream cheese
fresh orange juice

Place ingredients in a food processor bowl and process until smooth, adding enough orange juice for a thin drizzle.

Chocolate glaze:

½ cup semi-sweet chocolate chips
3 tbs. butter

1 tbs. light corn syrup

Combine ingredients in a small saucepan and stir over low heat until chocolate melts.

APPLE DOUBLE CHEESECAKE

Servings: 12

The unusual ingredient cheddar cheese makes this cheesecake different, but the flavor is so subtle that no one can quite figure out what you did. I've modified this by using apple pulp, but of course you can use poached sliced apples instead.

1 cup flour
1/4 cup sugar
1 tbs. grated lemon zest
1/2 cup butter
2 egg yolks, lightly beaten
1 tsp. vanilla
2 pkg. (8 oz. each) cream cheese,
   softened
4 oz. grated cheddar cheese
3/4 cup sugar

2 tbs. flour
2 eggs
1/4 cup milk
2 cups apple pulp
1 tbs. lemon juice
3/4 cup apple juice
1/4 cup sugar
1/4 tsp. cinnamon
1 tbs. cornstarch
1/2 tps. lemon extract

Preheat oven to 400°. Butter a 9-inch springform pan. Combine flour, sugar and lemon zest. Cut in butter and mix until crumbly. Add egg yolks and vanilla and mix well. Pat 1/2 of the dough on bottom of springform pan, remove sides of pan, and bake for 5 minutes. Pat remaining dough along sides of springform pan and attach to bottom. Dough should go half way up sides of pans. Set aside. Reduce oven to 375°. Using a food processor (preferably) or a mixer, beat together cream cheese, cheddar cheese, sugar, and flour until the mixture is smooth. Add eggs and beat until well blended and stir in milk. Pour into pastry-lined pan and bake for 35 to 40 minutes. Cool completely before applying glaze. In a saucepan, combine apple pulp, sugar and cinnamon together. Mix cornstarch with apple juice and lemon juice and add this to apple pulp mixture. Cook for approximately 5 minutes, adding additional apple juice if the mixture appears too thick. Remove from heat, add vanilla and let cool before adding to top of cake.

NOTE: The cake should be cooled thoroughly before serving, at least 4 hours, and can be made the day before.

MOIST APPLE CAKE

Serves: 12

I love this cake because it is so moist and actually tastes better the second day.

2 cups flour
2 cups sugar
2 tsp. baking soda
2 tsp. cinnamon
1 tsp. salt
4 cups apple pulp
1 cup chopped walnuts
2 eggs
½ cup vegetable oil

½ cup apple juice
2 tsp. vanilla
¼ cup butter
1 cup powdered sugar
1 tsp. vanilla extract
½ tsp. cinnamon
¼ tsp. nutmeg
½ cup apple juice

Preheat oven to 375°. Line a 9x13-inch pan with brown paper and butter paper and sides of pan. Mix flour, sugar, baking soda, cinnamon and salt together. Add apple pulp and walnuts. Stir in eggs, oil, apple juice and vanilla. Mix until well blended. Pour into prepared pans and bake for 45 minutes.

Make sauce: Heat butter, powdered sugar, vanilla, cinnamon, nutmeg and apple juice together and stir until thickened. Pour over warm cake.

NOTE: This cake can hold well for several days and can be frozen.

ORANGE CHEESECAKE

Servings: 12

This is a subtle creamy cheesecake that I like to serve after a luncheon or possibly with the addition of orange liqueur after an elegant dinner.

12 oz. premade ginger snap cookies
6 tbs. melted butter
1/2 cup chopped almonds
2 tbs. fresh orange juice
1 1/2 cups fresh orange juice
3-inch piece fresh ginger root

4 pkg. (8 oz. each) cream cheese, softened
2/3 cup sugar
1 tbs. minced orange zest
1 1/2 tsp. orange extract
8 oz. white chocolate, melted
4 large eggs

Place ginger snap cookies in a food processor and process until finely ground. Add melted butter, almonds and 2 tbs. orange juice (if desired you may add some orange zest for additional flavor). Press this mixture into bottom and 2 inches up sides of a 9-inch buttered springform pan. Preheat oven to 350°. Boil 1 1/2 cups fresh orange juice with ginger juice in a saucepan until mixture is reduced to about 1/4 cup, approximately 10 minutes. Beat cream cheese, sugar, orange zest and orange extract in food processor until smooth. Add reduced orange juice, mixing well. Add melted white chocolate and beat at a low speed. Add eggs one at a time, beating well. Pour batter into crust and bake until cheese cake puffs slightly, about 50 minutes. Cool and chill overnight.

STRAWBERRY PIE

Strawberry pie is a favorite of my parents. This glaze made from fresh strawberry juice creates a delicious flavor and makes a low calorie, high vitamin C dessert, wonderful to serve after a heavy meal.

one 9-inch prebaked pie shell
4 pints fresh strawberries
2 tbs. fresh orange juice
1 cup granulated sugar
3 tbs. cornstarch

1 tbs. butter
½ cup water
2 tbs. strawberry jam or jelly for
  glazing crust

Hull 3 pints of strawberries. Using your discretion, either leave strawberries whole or slice, and toss gently in a bowl with fresh orange juice. Take the remaining pint of strawberries and juice with the hulls. In a saucepan, mix strawberry juice with sugar, cornstarch and ½ cup of water and heat until mixture becomes thick. Add 1 tbs. butter. The mixture should be quite thick. Glaze bottom of baked pie crust with jam (this will help keep crust from becoming soggy). Fill crust with strawberries. Pour glaze over strawberries and refrigerate until well chilled. Serve with freshly whipped cream.

FRESH LEMON MERINGUE PIE

Servings: 8

Juicing lemons with the peel produces an intense flavor which makes this lemon meringue pie even better.

one 9-inch baked pie shell
1/3 cup cornstarch
1 1/2 cups sugar
1/4 tsp. salt
1 1/2 cups water
4 egg yolks, slightly beaten

1/3 cup fresh lemon juice
2 tbs. butter
4 egg whites
1/4 tsp. cream of tartar
1/2 cup sugar

In a saucepan, combine cornstarch, sugar and salt. Gradually add water, stirring until smooth. Bring mixture to a boil, stirring constantly, and boil for 1 minute. Remove from heat and quickly stir 1/2 of the hot mixture into egg yolks, mixing well. Return to saucepan and continue to cook over medium heat until mixture comes to a boil again; boil for approximately 1 minute longer. Remove from heat; stir in lemon juice and butter. Cool and pour into pie shell.

Preheat oven to 400°. Beat egg whites with cream of tartar until soft peaks form. Gradually beat in sugar a little at a time, beating well after each addition. Continue to beat until stiff peaks form. Spread meringue over cooled filling. Bake until golden brown on top. Let cool for 1 hour before serving.

APPLE ALLSPICE CAKE

Servings: 12

Another wonderful way to use both fresh apple juice and the apple pulp in a delicious moist cake.

2 cups flour
1 tbs. allspice
1½ tsp. cinnamon
2 tsp. baking powder
1 tsp. baking soda
¾ tsp. salt
¼ tsp. cloves
4 eggs
1¼ cups sugar
1 cup brown sugar, firmly packed
¾ cup vegetable oil

1 tbs. fresh lemon juice, with peel
3 cups apple pulp
½ cup fresh apple juice
1 cup chopped, toasted walnuts
1 cup fresh apple juice
½ cup cream
½ cup brown sugar
2 tbs. butter
¾ tsp. allspice
1 tsp. fresh lemon juice

Preheat oven to 350°. Butter a 9x13-inch pan. Combine flour, allspice, cinnamon, baking powder, baking soda, salt and cloves together in a separate bowl. Beat eggs, 1¼ cups sugar, brown sugar, oil and fresh lemon juice together in a bowl until very thick. Add flour mixture and combine until well blended. Stir in apple pulp, apple juice and walnuts. Pour into prepared pan and bake for approximately 1 hour. Pour 1 cup of fresh apple juice in a saucepan and boil until reduced to ½ cup. Add cream, brown sugar, butter and ¾ tsp. allspice and cook over medium high heat until mixture becomes thick, about 15 minutes. Remove from heat and add lemon juice. Pour this over hot cake and let cool for at least 1 hour in the pan.

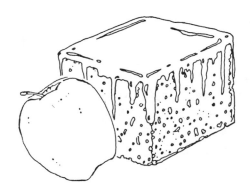

DILLY BREAD

I like this bread because it is very moist and can be varied by substituting alternative vegetable pulps.

1 tbs. yeast
½ cup warm water (115°)
1 cup cottage cheese
2 tbs. sugar
2 tbs. onion pulp
1 tbs. parsley pulp
1 tbs. butter

2 tsp. dill weed
1 tsp. salt
¼ tsp. baking soda
1 egg
2½ cups flour
butter
fresh garlic, minced, or garlic salt

Add yeast to water and let soften for 5 minutes. Add remaining ingredients and knead for 5 minutes; let rise for 1 hour. Form into a round loaf and place on a cookie sheet. Let rise until double in bulk. Bake in a 350° oven for 40 minutes. After removing from oven, spread generously with butter and sprinkle top with either fresh garlic or garlic salt.

CITRUS CAKE

A great combination of fresh grape juice, lemon juice and orange juice is used to glaze this delicious cake.

1½ cups butter
2½ cups sugar
8 eggs, separated
2 tsp. orange extract
1 tbs. lemon zest
1 tbs. orange zest

3 cups flour
½ cup fresh grapefruit juice
¼ cup fresh lemon juice, with peel
⅔ cup fresh orange juice
1 cup sugar
½ cup light rum

Preheat oven to 350°. Butter and flour a 10-inch tube cake pan. Cream together butter and sugar until fluffy. Add egg yolks one at a time, mixing well after each addition. Add orange extract, lemon zest and orange zest and mix well. Add flour and mix well. Whip egg whites until stiff and gently fold into batter until thoroughly combined. Pour into prepared pan and bake 1 hour. Remove from oven and invert onto a wire rack.

In a saucepan, mix grapefruit juice, lemon juice and orange juice together with sugar and heat until sugar dissolves. Remove from heat and add light rum. Brush this glaze over warm cake until all glaze is absorbed.

LEMON CREAM CHEESE MUFFINS

12 muffins

These are delightful breakfast muffins with a delicious lemon-flavored cream cheese center. For a change, I occasionally use a combination of both lemon and lime juices.

2 cups flour
1 tsp. baking soda
1/2 tsp. salt
1/2 cup sugar
2 eggs
1/2 cup fresh lemon juice, with peel

1/2 cup melted butter
1 tsp. vanilla
8 oz. cream cheese
1/2 cup sugar
4 tbs. fresh lemon juice

Preheat oven to 400° and butter 12 muffin cups. Whisk eggs, lemon juice, butter and vanilla together in a bowl. In a separate bowl, mix flour, baking soda, salt and sugar. Combine two mixtures and stir until barely mixed. Divide batter evenly among 12 cups. Using a mixer (or food processor), beat softened cream cheese with 1/2 cup sugar and 4 tbs. lemon juice until smooth. With the back of a spoon, press an indent into the top of each cup of batter and evenly distribute cream cheese mixture, placing a dollop in each indentation. Bake for 15 minutes, remove from oven and serve warm.

PINEAPPLE PIE

Pineapple pulp can be used in place of crushed pineapple in recipes, but the texture will change a little. This is a delicious way to use up your pulp and make something unusual.

2 tbs. flour
1/3 cup sugar
1/8 tsp. salt
2 egg yolks
1 cup pineapple juice
1/4 cup fresh orange juice

1 tsp. fresh lemon juice
1 1/4 cups pineapple pulp
2 tsp. butter
pastry for one 8-inch double crust
  pie

Preheat oven to 450°. In a saucepan, mix flour, sugar, and salt together; stir in beaten egg yolks along with pineapple juice, orange juice and lemon juice. Cook over medium heat until slightly thickened. Remove from heat and stir in pineapple pulp and butter. Line an 8-inch pie plate with pastry; brush with a little melted butter to prevent pie crust from getting soggy. Pour in filling and cover with top crust. Bake at 450° for 10 minutes; reduce to 350° and bake 25 minutes longer.

APPLE WALNUT RAISIN CAKE

Servings: 12

This is a wonderful moist spicy cake glazed with a whiskey sauce. Whenever I cook this everyone heads for the kitchen, and the cake doesn't last very long.

3 cups apple pulp
½ cup fresh apple juice
2 cups chopped walnuts
1 cup raisins
2 cups sugar
1½ cups vegetable oil
3 eggs
3 cups flour

1 tsp. baking soda
1 tsp. salt
1 tsp. cinnamon
1 tsp. sugar
1 cup dark brown sugar
½ cup butter
½ cup cream
¼ cup whiskey or apple brandy

Preheat oven to 350°. Mix apple pulp, apple juice, walnuts and raisins together and set aside. In a mixing bowl, add sugar, oil and eggs and beat until smooth. Sift dry ingredients together and add to egg mixture. Combine with apple-nut mixture and beat well. Pour into a buttered 9x13-inch pan and bake for 1 hour. Remove from oven and poke holes in top of cake with a fork. Combine dark brown sugar, butter, cream and whiskey together in a saucepan and heat until sugar dissolves, about 3 minutes. Pour glaze over warm cake and let cool.

LEMON TARTS

Lemon tarts are always a favorite at parties, especially tea parties.

2 cups sugar
1 cup fresh lemon juice
12 egg yolks

2 tbs. lemon zest
1 cup butter
8 prebaked tart shells

Place sugar, lemon juice and egg yolks in a mixer and beat until smooth. Pour mixture into a heavy-bottomed saucepan (or double boiler) and whisk mixture over heat until it thickens, approximately 15 minutes (it will take longer in double boiler). Remove thickened mixture from heat and stir in lemon zest and butter until completely melted. Pour into preheated, precooked tart shells and chill until firm.

NOTE: Another alternative is to sprinkle tops of tarts with a little granulated sugar and place under a broiler, watching carefully not to burn mixture. This will caramelize the tops and create a completely different taste sensation.

RAISED VEGETABLE BISCUITS

2 dozen

I added vegetable pulp to one of my favorite biscuit recipes and couldn't believe how much I liked it. These are great with a luncheon or served with a tea.

2 tbs. yeast
¼ cup warm water (115°)
2 tbs. sugar
4 cups flour
2 tsp. baking powder
2 tsp. salt

¼ cup butter
1¼ cups buttermilk
1 cup vegetable pulp (carrot, onion, celery, etc. or combination)
1½ tsp. herb seasoning (spike, or favorite combination of herbs)

Preheat oven to 425°. Mix yeast with warm water and sugar and stir until dissolved. Mix flour with baking powder and salt in a bowl. Cut in butter with a pastry blender until butter is the size of small peas. Add buttermilk and yeast mixture; mix until dough is moderately stiff. Add vegetable pulp and seasoning mix with a fork. Turn out on a floured board and knead slightly. Roll out to a thickness of ½ inch and cut into biscuits, placing them on a greased pan so that they just barely touch each other. Brush with a little melted butter and prick with a fork. Let rise until double in bulk. Bake for approximately 12 minutes. These are best served warm.

LEMON CHIFFON PIE

This is another delicious way to use fresh lemon juice.

one 9-inch prebaked pie crust
1 envelope unflavored gelatin
3/4 cup fresh lemon juice
4 egg yolks
3/4 cup sugar
1 tbs. finely grated lime zest
3 egg whites
1 cup cream, whipped and flavored with a little sugar

Mix gelatin with 1/4 of the lemon juice and set aside to soften. In a heavy saucepan, combine egg yolks, sugar, remaining lemon juice and lemon zest. Cook, stirring constantly, until mixture thickens and coats the back of a spoon. Do not boil. Dissolve gelatin over low heat and stir into lemon mixture. Place saucepan in a bowl of ice and stir until mixture begins to thicken. Beat egg whites until stiff. Stir 1/4 of the egg whites into lemon mixture to lighten; fold in remaining whites. Pour into prepared pie shell and refrigerate for at least 3 hours before serving. Whip cream, add sugar to taste and spread on top of chilled pie mixture before serving.

ORANGE CHIFFON CAKE

Servings: 12

Sometimes in the place of angel food cake I like to make chiffon cakes. Orange chiffon is a great alternative, especially when smothered with a pineapple whipped cream frosting.

2¼ cups sifted flour
¾ cup sugar
1 tbs. baking powder
½ tsp. salt
½ cup vegetable oil
7 egg yolks

1 cup fresh orange juice
2 tbs. orange zest
2 tsp. orange extract
9 egg whites
1 tsp. cream of tartar
¾ cup sugar

Preheat oven to 325°. Mix together flour, sugar, baking powder and salt. In a separate bowl, whisk oil, egg yolks, orange juice, orange zest and orange extract. Mix egg-orange mixture into flour mixture until batter is smooth. In a large bowl, beat egg whites until foamy, add cream of tartar and beat until they hold soft peaks. Add ¾ cup sugar and beat until egg whites hold stiff glossy peaks. Stir ⅓ of the stiff whites into batter to lighten it and then fold in the remaining whites. Spoon batter into an ungreased 10-inch tube pan with a removable bottom. Bake for 55 minutes or until tester comes out clean. Invert pan immediately onto a rack and let cake cool completely while upside down.

Run a long thin knife around the outer edge of pan to remove cake. With a serrated knife make 2 horizontal cuts through the cake so that you end up with 3 layers of cake. Cover layers and outside of cake with frosting. Refrigerate until ready to serve.

PINEAPPLE PARFAIT FROSTING
2 cups heavy cream
1 tsp. orange extract
¼ cup sugar
1 large can crushed pineapple, well drained

Whip cream in a large bowl and add orange extract and sugar. Fold in pineapple.

APPLE PEANUT BUTTER BREAD

1 loaf

Kids are crazy about this; I like it because it stays moist so long.

½ cup dark brown sugar
½ cup sugar
½ cup vegetable oil
¼ cup peanut butter
2 cups apple pulp
2 tbs. fresh apple juice

2 tsp. cinnamon
2 cups flour
1 tsp. baking soda
½ tsp. salt
2 eggs
1 cup nuts (peanuts, walnuts, etc.)

Preheat oven to 350°. Mix sugars and oil together and beat in peanut butter until well combined. In a separate bowl, mix apple pulp with apple juice and cinnamon and set aside. Mix flour, baking soda, and salt together and set aside. To the sugar mixture add eggs one at a time, beating well after each addition. Beat in flour mixture until just combined. Stir in apple mixture and nuts. Pour into a brown paper-lined, buttered loaf pan and bake for 45 minutes or until tester comes out clean.

VEGETABLE COOKIES

A great way to use either your carrot or zucchini pulps. Sometimes I like to glaze these with an orange icing.

2/3 cup butter
1 1/4 cups dark brown sugar
2 eggs
1 tsp. vanilla
1 tbs. grated lemon zest
1/2 cup buttermilk
2 cups flour
1 tsp. baking powder
1 tsp. baking soda

1 tsp. salt
1 1/2 tsp. cinnamon
1/4 nutmeg
2 cups oatmeal
1 cup raisins
1/2 cup chopped walnuts
2 cups vegetable pulp (carrot or zucchini)
1/2 cup carrot juice

Preheat oven to 400°. Cream together butter and brown sugar. Add eggs, vanilla, lemon zest and buttermilk and beat. Mix together flour, baking powder, baking soda, salt, cinnamon and nutmeg. Add dry ingredients to butter mixture. Stir in oats, raisins, nuts, vegetable pulp and carrot juice. Drop by tablespoons onto a greased cookie sheet. Bake about 12 minutes.

LIME CAKE

A great way to use lime juice to create a unique cake that is coated with a delicious lime syrup.

2⅔ cups flour
1 tbs. baking powder
½ tsp. salt
½ cup butter
1½ cups sugar
3 eggs, lightly beaten

1 tbs. lime zest
3 tbs. fresh lime juice (with peel)
1 cup buttermilk
1½ cups powdered sugar
¾ cup fresh lime juice (with peel)

Preheat oven to 350°. Butter a bundt pan and set aside. Mix together flour, baking powder and salt; set aside. Beat together butter and sugar until well blended. Gradually beat in eggs. Beat in lime zest and lime juice. Add flour mixture alternately with buttermilk. Spoon batter into prepared pan and bake 45 minutes, or until tester inserted comes out clean.

To make syrup: Mix together powdered sugar and lime juice with a whisk until sugar dissolves. While cake is still warm, pierce top of cake with fork or a skewer and pour lime juice over cake until all juice is absorbed. Just before serving, sprinkle cake with a little powdered sugar.

LEMON SOUFFLÉ

Lemon soufflé is one of my favorite desserts. I like it because it is so light and can be served after a heavy meal.

2 tbs. butter
2 tbs. flour
½ cup half and half
⅓ cup fresh lemon juice (with peel)
⅓ cup sugar

2 tbs. lemon zest
5 egg yolks
5 egg whites
⅛ tsp. cream of tartar
⅛ tsp. salt

Preheat oven to 400°. Butter and sugar a 1-quart soufflé dish. Cut a piece of parchment or waxed paper long enough to go around the dish and fold paper in half lengthwise. Brush sides of paper with butter and sprinkle with sugar. Tie paper around the dish with buttered side turned inward and extending 2 inches above the rim. Melt butter, stir in flour and cook for 2 minutes. Remove from heat and stir in half and half. Return to heat and cook until thick. With pan removed from heat, beat in lemon juice, sugar, lemon zest and egg yolks. Cool. Beat egg whites until foamy; add cream of tartar and salt. Beat until eggs are stiff but not dry. Spoon into prepared soufflé dish and place on the middle shelf of oven. Reduce heat to 375° and bake for 35 minutes. Serve immediately.

ZUCCHINI NUT LOAF

1 loaf

I'm always looking for new ways to work with zucchini and this is well appreciated, even by kids who hate zucchini!

2½ cups flour, white or whole wheat
2 tsp. baking powder
1 tsp. baking soda
1 tbs. lemon zest
¾ tsp. salt
½ tsp. cinnamon
¼ tsp. ginger

2 beaten eggs
1¼ cups sugar
½ cup vegetable oil
2 cups zucchini pulp
½ cup fresh orange juice
1 cup chopped walnuts

Preheat oven to 350°. Stir together flour, baking powder, baking soda, lemon zest, salt, cinnamon and ginger; set aside. Beat together eggs, sugar and oil. Add this to flour mixture and beat well. Next add zucchini pulp, orange juice and walnuts and mix well. Line a loaf pan with brown paper; butter lightly. Bake for 50 minutes or until a knife inserted in the center comes out clean.

ORANGE DATE BARS

18 bars

Date bars are a favorite cookie, especially around holiday time. I think these are much better when made with fresh orange juice.

1½ cups chopped pitted dates
1½ cups fresh orange juice
2½ cups flour
½ tsp. salt
1½ cups dark brown sugar,
  firmly packed

1½ cups butter
1 cup coconut
1 cup walnuts
1½ cups oatmeal

Preheat oven to 350°. In a heavy saucepan, simmer dates and orange juice for 30 minutes, until dates are soft and mixture is thick. Mix flour and salt together; set aside. Combine brown sugar and butter together and beat until well mixed. Add flour mixture and beat. Add coconut, walnuts and oatmeal and mix until crumbly.

Press half of the crumb mixture into a well-greased 9x13-inch pan. Spread date mixture on top and cover with remaining crumb mixture. Bake for 45 minutes or until golden. Cool and cut into bars.

LEMON ANGEL WHISPERS

You'll be impressed with the melt-in-your-mouth quality of these special cookies.

1 cup butter
1 cup margarine
1 cup powdered sugar
2 tsp. lemon extract
4 cups flour
½ tsp. salt

2 eggs, slightly beaten
2 tbs. lemon zest
1⅓ cups sugar
6 tbs. fresh lemon juice
3 tbs. soft butter

Preheat oven to 400°. Cream butter and margarine together and add sugar, beating until fluffy. Add lemon extract, flour and salt; blend well. Chill dough for at least 1 hour. Roll dough into small balls and place on an ungreased cookie sheet about 1 inch apart. Flatten slightly. Bake for 8 to 10 minutes, until the edges are slightly brown. Cool.

Blend eggs, lemon zest, sugar, lemon juice and butter together and cook over medium heat, stirring constantly, until mixture becomes thick. Chill until firm. Place one teaspoon of the filling between 2 cooled cookies.

ENTRÉES AND SIDE DISHES

ORANGE FRENCH TOAST

Servings: 4

*I'm always looking for an alternative to the typical breakfast menu and Orange French Toast is a nice change. It's especially good served with **Blueberry Sauce,** page 59.*

8 beaten eggs
1 tbs. orange zest
¾ cup fresh orange juice
¼ tsp. cinnamon
½ cup half and half, or cream
8 thick slices of egg bread
butter

Combine eggs, orange zest, orange juice, cinnamon and half and half or cream, and blend until smooth. Soak bread slices in egg mixture until it is well absorbed and sauté slowly in butter in a skillet. I usually baste French toast with a little extra egg mixture when I first start to sauté. Turn and sauté the other side until golden brown. Serve topped with maple syrup, fruited syrups or sauces.

APPLE FRENCH TOAST

Servings: 4

This is a new twist to French toast that includes apple juice in the egg mixture. The toast is served with an apple pulp sauce.

8 eggs
1 cup fresh apple juice
1/3 cup half and half
2 tsp. sugar
1 tsp. cinnamon
pinch of salt

8 thick slices of egg bread
4 tbs. butter
1/4 cup sugar, or more to taste
1 cup apple pulp, without seeds or
   stems
1/4 cup dark rum, optional

Whisk eggs, apple juice, half and half, sugar, cinnamon and salt together and pour over bread slices, allowing them to soak for 10 minutes. Melt butter in a skillet and stir in sugar and apple pulp. Cook for a few minutes and taste, adjusting sugar to your personal preference. Add rum if desired. Sauté well-soaked bread until golden brown, turning once. Serve apple pulp sauce over toast.

NOTE: When working with apple pulp, you must watch to remove any large pieces of apple peeling that may have not been chopped finely enough.

CHILI

5 quarts

Chili is a great way to use tomato juice for those times of the year when the tomato crop is abundant.

1½ lbs. dried small chili beans
2 lbs. ground beef
salt and pepper to taste
1-2 tsp. Worcestershire sauce
3½ tbs. chili powder
1 tbs. salt, or to taste
3 tbs. cumin
2 tsp. red pepper flakes
8 garlic cloves, minced
3 cups fresh tomato juice
15 oz. tomato paste

If using dried beans, soak beans overnight in water. Drain soaked beans and be certain to sort out any foreign particles such as little pebbles. Put beans in a pan and cover with water. Bring to a boil, stirring occasionally. Fry ground beef until well done, crumbling and adding salt and pepper to taste. Add Worcestershire sauce, chili powder, salt, cumin, red pepper flakes and garlic. When beans have cooked until softened, add tomato juice. Bring mixture to a boil and add tomato paste. Stir. Let mixture come to a boil again and thicken slightly, about 5 to 10 minutes. Add ground beef and simmer until flavors have developed, about 15 to 20 minutes. You may need to add some water to the mixture if it appears too thick. Taste and adjust seasonings to your personal preference.

NOTE: You may use 3 (1 lb. each) cans chili beans in place of dried chili beans.

SPAGHETTI SAUCE

3 quarts

My friend Peggy makes a great quick spaghetti sauce that I adapted using vegetable pulps.

1½ lbs. ground beef
8 Italian sausages, cut into
   ½-inch slices
2 garlic cloves, minced
¼ cup chopped parsley
¼ cup onion pulp
¼ cup celery pulp
¼ cup green pepper pulp
½ lb. fresh mushrooms, sliced
1 can (6 oz.) tomato paste
1 can (8 oz.) tomato sauce

1 can (1 lb.) tomatoes
½ cup water
½ cup red wine
1 tbs. oregano
1 tbs. sugar, or to taste
1 tbs. basil
1 tbs. chili powder
1 tbs. cumin
1 tbs. paprika
salt and pepper to taste

Brown beef and sausages in a Dutch oven or heavy saucepan and drain off fat. Add garlic, onion pulp, celery pulp and green pepper pulp to pan and cook until tender. Add remaining ingredients. Cover and cook slowly for 1 hour. Taste and adjust seasonings to personal preference.

STUFFED ROUND STEAK

Servings: 6

You can create endless new dishes with this recipe by varying the types of pulps used and the spices, so that you never get tired of the same old dish.

3 lbs. round steaks
salt, pepper and paprika to taste
1/4 lb. sliced mushrooms
1/2 cup onion pulp, or to taste
1 small jar pimientos, or 1/4 cup red
  bell pepper pulp
1 1/2 cups bread crumbs

1 cup melted butter
1 tbs. boiling water
1 egg
stuffed olives, optional
1/2 cup flour
1/4 cup melted butter for browning
l cup red wine

Pound round steaks until thin. Rub in salt, pepper and plenty of paprika. Overlap meat so that it makes one large steak. Spread meat with sliced mushrooms, onion pulp and pimiento or red pepper pulp. Cover with bread crumbs. Mix butter, boiling water and egg together and dribble this mixture over bread crumbs. You may wish to arrange a row of stuffed olives along the side of the steak. Begin the roll of the meat around the olives and tie firmly. Flour outside of meat roll and brown in 1/4 cup of melted butter. Place in a foil-lined roasting pan. Sprinkle outside with salt, pepper and paprika and add red wine. Roast meat in a 350° oven for about 2 hours. Serve hot or cold.

ORANGE PORK MEDALLIONS

Servings: 6

Pork tenderloin is a great fast meal to fix because the meat is so tender and the recipe requires such a short period of time to prepare.

3 pork tenderloins
2 tbs. butter
salt and pepper to taste
3 garlic cloves, minced
¾ cup white wine
1 cup fresh orange juice

1 tbs. flour
2 tbs. water
1 tbs. Dijon mustard
2 tbs. minced parsley
1 tbs. orange zest
orange slices for garnish

Melt butter in a heavy skillet. Cut pork tenderloin into ½-inch slices and fry in butter with minced garlic. Brown each side very lightly. Add wine and orange juice. Simmer for a few minutes and remove to a warm plate. Make a paste of flour and water and stir into pan with meat juices until thickened. Add Dijon mustard, minced garlic, orange zest and cooked tenderloins. Stir until meat is covered with sauce and serve immediately.

LEMON PEPPER CHICKEN

Servings: 2

Here is a marinade for chicken that can be made quickly. I enjoy it when I'm in a hurry because, after the chicken marinates all day, I come home and simply broil or bake it and dinner is ready in a flash.

½ cup fresh lemon juice, with peel
4 garlic cloves, minced
1 tbs. onion pulp
1 tsp. thyme

2 bay leaves
1 cup olive oil
1-2 tsp. black pepper
2½ lb. chicken, halved

In a bowl, blend together lemon juice, garlic, onion pulp, thyme, bay leaves, olive oil and pepper. Split chicken in half or cut into pieces and place in marinade. Cover and chill for at least 2 hours. Arrange chicken on a roasting pan and baste with some of the marinade. Bake in a 450° oven for 35 to 45 minutes or until meat is done. Test for doneness by sticking a fork or a skewer into the thigh to see if the juices run clear.

COCONUT CHICKEN

This is a really quick meal that's easy to fix. The only unusual ingredient is fish sauce which can be located at most Oriental supply stores.

½ lb. boneless chicken breast
½-1 tsp. red pepper flakes
1-3 tbs. fresh lemon juice
1 tbs. fresh lime juice
2 tbs. vegetable oil
½ cup coconut milk

½ tsp. salt
2 to 3 tbs. fish sauce
15 sweet basil leaves, fresh
1 tbs. cornstarch, or more if needed
2 cups chopped cabbage

Cut chicken into strips. Sauté chicken in oil for a few minutes and add lemon juice, lime juice, coconut milk and salt. Cook for a few minutes until chicken is done. Stir in fish sauce and basil and cook for 1 minute longer. Taste and adjust to your personal preference. Add a little water to cornstarch to make into a paste and stir into chicken mixture. Cook until mixture thickens. Taste and adjust seasonings again.

NOTE: The quantity of lemon juice, lime juice and fish sauce is really according to personal preference and you need to consider that when you are adjusting the seasoning, so start out with a small quantity and adjust up.

QUICK LEMON CHICKEN

Servings: 4 to 6

This is a fast easy way to make a sauce to serve over chicken strips.

3 lbs. chicken breast, boned and
  skinned
¼ cup fresh lemon juice
2 tbs. butter
1 tbs. vegetable oil
1 garlic clove, minced
⅓ cup chicken stock

2 tsp. cornstarch
1 tbs. sugar
1 tsp. soy sauce
1 tbs. water
salt to taste
lemon slices for garnish

Cut chicken into half-inch strips. Place butter and oil in a skillet and quickly fry chicken strips until just barely cooked. Remove chicken strips to a plate. Add lemon juice, garlic, chicken stock, soy sauce and sugar to pan and stir. Mix cornstarch in water and add to pan. Heat mixture until it thickens. Taste and adjust flavors to personal preference. Add sauce to chicken strips and stir until heated through. Garnish with lemon slices.

VEGETABLE STUFFED CHICKEN BREASTS   Servings: 4

This recipe was converted using celery and onion pulps but you can use almost any vegetable pulp to change this as long as you taste and adjust seasonings to your personal preference.

4 whole chicken breasts
salt and pepper to taste
rosemary
¼ cup butter
2 tbs. minced parsley

2 tbs. onion pulp
⅓ cup celery pulp
½ cup bread crumbs
1 tsp. rosemary
1 tbs. white wine, optional

Bone chicken breasts, leaving skin on, and cut in half. Flatten slightly with a rolling pin or a meat tenderizer. Sprinkle each breast with a little salt, pepper and rosemary. In a skillet, melt butter and add parsley, onion pulp and celery pulp. Stir for 1 to 2 minutes, adding a little water if it appears too dry. Stir in bread crumbs, add rosemary and taste. If this mixture seems a little dry, add white wine if desired. Divide stuffing into 8 equal portions and stuff each breast. Fold each breast skin side up into a little bundle and place on a lightly greased casserole dish. Bake in a 400° oven for approximately 30 minutes. Test for doneness.

CRISP ROAST DUCK WITH CUMBERLAND SAUCE

Servings: 6

My sister-in-law Christie loves duck and developed this recipe, which makes people who don't like duck change their minds.

2 ducks (approximately 5 lbs. each)
2 tbs. red currant jelly
⅔ cup fresh orange juice
½ orange, finely chopped

1 tbs. grated orange zest
½ cup currants
½ cup light corn syrup
½ cup butter

Place ducks in a shallow roasting pan and refrigerate, uncovered, for 1 to 2 days to dry out skin. Bring ducks to room temperature at least 2 hours before roasting. Preheat oven to 500°. Remove giblets and pull out any fat from cavities. Prick skin with a fork at ½-inch intervals all over breast and legs. Line a deep roasting pan with aluminium and place ducks (breast side down) on a rack in pan. Roast ducks for 25 to 30 minutes. Remove fat from pan. Turn breast side up and continue roasting for 30 more minutes, removing fat every 15 minutes. The skin should be very crisp and deep golden brown. In a saucepan, place red currant jelly, orange pieces, orange zest, currants, corn syrup and butter. Bring to a boil and simmer for 15 minutes. Serve over roasted duck slices.

DILLED SALMON

Servings: 12

I like a lightly flavored sauce to serve over salmon so that you can enjoy the true salmon flavor. This sauce can also be served on other fish such as red snapper or even cod.

¼ cup red vinegar (I prefer balsamic)
¼ cup fresh lemon juice, with peel
1 tsp. dill weed
½ tsp. black pepper
1 tsp. salt

1 cup cream
1 cup sour cream
12 (8 oz. each) salmon fillets
fresh dill for garnish, if available

In a saucepan, combine vinegar, lemon juice, dill weed, black pepper and salt and simmer for 5 minutes. Blend cream, sour cream and vinegar mixture together. Place fillets on a buttered baking dish and pour the mixture over them. Bake at 350° for approximately 20 minutes. Serve hot or cold.

NOTE: The standard cooking time for fish is based on measuring the fish at the thickest portion of the fillet or whole fish. For every inch of thickness, cook the fish 10 minutes.

MEDITERRANEAN GREEN BEANS

Servings: 6 to 8

It may seem a little strange using something like anchovies to flavor a vegetable, but you will really be surprised at how much you will enjoy this dish.

1 lb. fresh green beans
¼ cup olive oil
1 to 2 garlic cloves
1 can anchovies
2 tbs. fresh lemon juice, with peel
black pepper to taste

Cook beans until tender, drain and refresh in cold water to stop the cooking process. Drain again, dry beans and set aside. In a large skillet, heat olive oil and add whole garlic cloves. Cook garlic until it just turns brown and discard. Add beans to pan and cook, turning to coat and to brown slightly. Remove beans and set aside. Place anchovies in pan, mashing with a fork. Add lemon juice to mixture and heat until bubbly. Pour over beans and toss to coat. Add black pepper to taste.

MOCK SPINACH SOUFFLÉ

Servings: 10 to 12

This is a family favorite that I quite often take with me when asked to bring a vegetable dish to a party.

2 cans (13¾ oz. each) artichoke hearts, drained and quartered
1 pkg. Italian salad dressing mix
½ cup oil (olive or combination of oils)
¼ cup vinegar (I prefer balsamic)

¼ cup fresh lemon juice
2 pkg. (8 oz. each) cream cheese
2 tbs. mayonnaise
6 pkg. (10½ oz. each) frozen chopped spinach
1½ cups grated Parmesan cheese

Preheat oven to 350°. Butter a casserole or soufflé dish. Mix Italian dressing mix with oil, vinegar and lemon juice. Pour on artichoke hearts and let them marinate while preparing remaining ingredients. Thaw and thoroughly drain frozen chopped spinach (squeeze spinach so that it is quite dry). Mix cream cheese with mayonnaise until smooth. Place ⅓ of the spinach mixture on bottom of casserole dish. Place ⅓ of the artichokes on top of spinach with a little marinade for flavor. Spread ⅓ of the cream cheese on top of artichokes and repeat whole process two more times. Top with a very heavy layer of grated Parmesan. Bake for 45 minutes and serve hot.

PINEAPPLE BAKE

Servings: 4 to 6

My sister-in-law Christie introduced this to me as an alternative to rice pilaf when cooking a tropical dinner. I personally feel it is far better than poi!

4 slices white bread with crust
½ cup melted butter
½ cup sugar
3 eggs
3 tbs. flour
1½ cups pineapple pulp, without peel
¼ cup fresh pineapple juice

Preheat oven to 350°. Process bread in a food processor or blender to make crumbs and toss with melted butter. Combine sugar, eggs, flour, pineapple pulp and pineapple juice and pour into a buttered casserole dish. Top with buttered crumbs and bake for 1 hour.

CARROT CUSTARD

This is a beautiful presentation for a carrot dish in which the carrots are sliced and placed in spiral design in the bottom of a pie pan. The filling made from carrot pulp is poured on top and baked and then this is cut into pie-shaped wedges for serving.

4 large carrots, sliced
1 tbs. butter
3 cups carrot pulp
1-1½ cup water, or carrot juice
⅓ cup brown sugar
3 beaten eggs

¼ cup sour cream
2 tbs. orange zest
1 tsp. salt
¼ tsp. cinnamon, or to taste
¼ tsp. ginger
¼ tsp. cloves

Cook and steam carrots until tender; cool. Using 1 tbs. of butter, butter bottom of either a quiche pan or pie pan and arrange cooled carrot slices in concentric circles on bottom. Cook carrot pulp in water or carrot juice until tender. Drain off any excess moisture. Combine remaining ingredients and process in a blender or food processor until smooth. Pour mixture on top of arranged carrot slices. Bake at 350° for 45 minutes. Let stand briefly before cutting into wedges.

LEMON RISOTTO

Lemon adds a real zest to this cheese-flavored Italian rice dish and it is particularly good served with fish meals.

3 tbs. butter
2 tbs. olive oil
1/4 cup onion pulp
1 tbs. lemon zest
1½ cups rice
4½ cups chicken stock
1/3 cup fresh lemon juice
½ cup grated Parmesan cheese
salt and pepper to taste

Melt butter in a saucepan and add olive oil. Add onion pulp and lemon zest; sauté for 3 minutes. Add rice and stir for several minutes until rice begins to take on a slightly brown color. Add chicken stock and lemon juice; simmer until rice is tender. Gently stir in Parmesan cheese and season with salt and pepper. Serve immediately.

APPLE RED CABBAGE

Apples are a great accompaniment to cabbage and I particularly like them in a sweet and sour mixture. Serve this with pork, beef or sausage.

3 tbs. butter
2 tbs. onion pulp
¼ cup vinegar
3 tbs. brown sugar
salt and pepper to taste
¾-1 cup apple pulp
1 small red cabbage, coarsely shredded

In a frying pan, heat butter and sauté onion until soft, about 2 to 3 minutes. Add vinegar, sugar, salt and pepper to taste. Add apple pulp and cabbage. If mixture is too dry, add a little water or apple juice. Cover and cook until cabbage wilts, approximately 10 minutes. Taste and adjust to personal taste for tartness or sweetness.

RICE AND FRUIT STUFFING

4 cups

This is a great stuffing for roast chicken or turkey. The apples and oranges give this an unusual flavor that surprises your guests.

1 tbs. vegetable oil
2 tbs. butter
2 tbs. onion pulp
1 cup long grain rice
1½ cups hot water
½ cup fresh orange juice

salt and pepper to taste
½ cup apple pulp
½ cup raisins
½ tsp. cinnamon
½ cup toasted slivered almonds

In a skillet, heat oil and butter. Add onion, stirring until tender, about 3 minutes. Increase heat, add rice and sauté until slightly brown. Add water, orange juice, salt and pepper, and bring to a boil. Reduce heat, cover and cook for 10 minutes. Add apple pulp, raisins and cinnamon and cook for 2 minutes. Taste and adjust seasonings to your personal preference. Just before serving, add toasted slivered almonds.

APPENDIX A: JUICE YIELDS

So you can have an idea of the quantity of produce to buy for your recipes, I am including this section on juice yields. Produce varies considerably in size and also in water content, so please be aware that these are only approximate measures.

PRODUCE	QUANTITY	JUICE YIELD
apples	2 medium	1 cup
apricots	1 pound	1 cup
asparagus	4 large stalks	1/4 cup
beans, green	1/2 pound	1/3 cup
beets	3 whole	1/2 cup
blackberries	1 cup	1/2 cup
broccoli	6 ounces	1/4 cup
cabbage	1 pound	1/2 cup
cantaloupe	1 small	1 cup
carrots	3 large	1 cup
celery	3 stalks	1/2 cup
cherries	1 pound	3/4 cup
coconut meat	12 ounces	1/4 cup

PRODUCE	QUANTITY	JUICE YIELD
cranberries	2 cups	½ cup
cucumber	1 medium	½ cup
grapefruit	1 medium	½ cup
grapes	1 pound	1 cup
honeydew melon	1 medium	1¼ cups
kiwi	1 medium	2 tbs.
leek	1 medium	2 tbs.
lemon	1 medium	2 tbs.
lettuce	3 leaves	1 tbs.
lime	1 medium	1 tbs.
mango	1 medium	½ cup
nectarines	3 medium	¾ cup
onion	3 large	½ cup
orange	4 medium	1 cup
papaya	1 medium	½ cup
parsley	1 wad	1 tbs.
peach	1 medium	¼
pear	1 large	¾ cup

PRODUCE	QUANTITY	JUICE YIELD
pepper, bell	1 medium	1/3 cup
pineapple	3/4-inch slice	1/2 cup
plums	8 medium	1 cup
potato	1 medium	1/2 cup
potato, red	3 medium	3/4 cup
radishes	4 ounces	1/4 cup
raspberries	2 cups	3/4 cup
rhubarb	1 medium stalk	1/3 cup
spinach	1 pound	2/3 cup
sprouts, alfalfa	1 pkg. (5 oz.)	3 tbs.
sprouts, bean	8 ounces	2/3 cup
strawberries	16 berries	1/2 cup
tangerine	1 medium	3 tbs.
tomato	2 large	1 cup
watermelon	12 ounce slice with rind	1 cup
zucchini	8 ounces	1/2 cup

APPENDIX B: TYPICAL GROWING SEASON

PRODUCE	JAN	FEB	MAR	APR	MAY	JUNE	JULY	AUG	SEPT	OCT	NOV	DEC
apple								x	x	x	x	x
apricot			x	x	x	x						
asparagus			x	x	x							
beans, green						x	x	x	x	x	x	
beet						x	x	x	x	x	x	
blackberry							x	x				
blueberry							x	x				
broccoli							x	x	x	x		
cabbage								x	x	x	x	x
cantaloupe					x	x	x	x	x	x		
carrot							x	x	x	x	x	
celery								x	x	x	x	
cherry				x	x	x	x	x				
coconut	x	x	x	x	x	x	x	x	x	x	x	x
cranberry										x	x	x
cucumber								x	x	x		
grapefruit	x	x	x	x	x							

PRODUCE	JAN	FEB	MAR	APR	MAY	JUNE	JULY	AUG	SEPT	OCT	NOV	DEC
grapes					X	X	X	X	X	X	X	X
honeydew				X	X	X	X	X	X	X		
kiwi						X	X	X	X			
leek	X	X	X	X								
lemon				X	X	X	X	X				
lettuce						X	X	X	X	X		
lime						X	X	X	X	X		
mango						X	X	X	X			
nectarine						X	X	X	X			
onion						X	X	X	X	X		
orange				X	X	X	X	X	X	X		
papaya						X	X	X	X	X		
parsley						X	X	X	X			
peach						X	X	X				
pear	X	X	X	X	X	X						
peppers, bell									X	X	X	
pineapple				X	X	X						
plum						X	X	X	X			
potato	X	X	X	X		X	X	X	X	X	X	

PRODUCE	JAN	FEB	MAR	APR	MAY	JUNE	JULY	AUG	SEPT	OCT	NOV	DEC
potato, red						X	X	X	X	X	X	X
radishes					X	X	X	X	X	X		
raspberry									X	X	X	X
rhubarb				X	X	X	X	X	X			
spinach				X	X	X	X	X	X	X	X	
sprouts, alf.	X	X	X	X	X	X	X	X	X	X	X	X
sprout, bean	X	X	X	X	X	X	X	X	X	X	X	X
strawberry						X	X					
tangerine	X	X	X									X
tomato								X	X			
watermelon						X	X	X	X			
zucchini							X	X	X	X		

APPENDIX C: CALORIE CONTENT OF PRODUCE

PRODUCE	QUANTITY	CALORIES (raw)
alfalfa sprouts	1 cup	8
apple	1 medium	80
apricot	3 medium	55
artichoke	1 pound	85
asparagus	1 cup	35
avocado	½ each	185
banana	1 medium	101
beans, green	1 cup	26
beet greens	½ cup	13
beets	1 cup	54
bell pepper	1 each	40
blackberries	1 cup	84
blueberries	1 cup	90
broccoli	1 cup	40
Brussels sprouts	1 cup	56

PRODUCE	QUANTITY	CALORIES (raw)
cabbage	1 cup	22
cantaloupe	1 cup	48
carrot	1 medium	30
cauliflower	1 cup	31
celery	1 cup	20
cherries	1 cup	102
coconut	1 cup	277
collard greens	1 cup	63
corn	1 ear	70
cranberries	1 cup	44
cucumber	1 cup	35
dates	1 cup	542
eggplant	1 cup	48
figs	1 each	30
garlic	1 clove	4
ginger root	½ inch	10
grapefruit	1 medium	80
grapes	1 cup	107

PRODUCE	QUANTITY	CALORIES (raw)
kale	½ pound	77
lemon	1 medium	20
lettuce	1 cup	10
lima beans	1 cup	189
lime	1 medium	15
mushroom	1 cup	20
mustard greens	1 cup	32
okra	4 ounces	35
onion	1 cup	65
orange	1 medium	71
papaya	1 cup	71
parsley	1 cup	26
parsnip	½ cup	70
peach	1 medium	58
pear	1 medium	100
peas	1 cup	114
pineapple	1 cup	81
plums	1 cup	87

PRODUCE	QUANTITY	CALORIES (raw)
potato	1 medium	145
prunes	1 cup	344
pumpkin	1 cup	81
radishes	1 cup	20
raspberries	1 cup	70
rhubarb	1 cup	20
spinach	1 cup	14
sprouts, bean	½ pound	80
squash, wntr.	1 cup	93
strawberries	1 cup	55
sweet potato	1 medium	172
Swiss chard	½ cup	17
tangerine	1 medium	39
tomato	1 medium	27
turnip	½ cup	20
watercress	½ cup	3
watermelon	1 cup	42
wheatgrass	1 cup	7
zucchini	1 cup	22

APPENDIX D: VITAMIN CONTENT OF PRODUCE

PRODUCE	A	B-1	B-2	B-3	B-5	B-6	B-12	C	D	E	F	K	P
alfalfa sprouts	x	x	x	x	x	x	x	x	x	x		x	
apple	x		x					x					
apricot	x		x	x				x					x
artichoke	x			x				x					
asparagus	x	x	x	x				x		x			
avocado	x	x	x	x	x	x			x	x	x		
banana	x		x	x		x		x					
beans, green	x		x	x			x	x					
beet greens	x							x					
beets	x					x		x					
bell pepper	x					x		x					
blackberries	x							x					x
blueberries	x							x					
broccoli	x	x	x		x			x		x			
Brussels sprouts	x		x					x					

PRODUCE	A	B-1	B-2	B-3	B-5	B-6	B-12	C	D	E	F	K	P
cabbage	x				x	x		x				x	
cantaloupe	x					x		x					
carrot	x				x				x	x		x	
cauliflower					x			x				x	
celery	x							x					
cherries	x		x					x					x
coconut													
collard greens	x	x	x					x					
corn		x	x	x		x				x		x	
cranberries	x							x					
cucumber	x							x					
dates		x	x	x									
eggplant													
figs		x	x	x									
garlic	x	x	x	x			x	x	x		x		
ginger root											x	x	
grapefruit	x							x					x
grapes	x							x					x

PRODUCE	A	B-1	B-2	B-3	B-5	B-6	B-12	C	D	E	F	K	P
kale	x							x				x	
lemon						x		x					x
lettuce	x							x		x		x	
lima beans	x	x	x					x					
lime								x					
mushroom				x	x				x			x	
mustard greens	x		x					x					
okra	x	x	x					x					
onion		x	x	x	x			x					x
orange	x				x	x		x		x	x		x
papaya	x							x					
parsley	x	x	x	x				x		x			x
parsnip	x												
peach	x							x					
pear	x	x	x					x					x
peas	x	x		x	x	x		x					
pineapple	x							x					
plum	x												x

PRODUCE	A	B-1	B-2	B-3	B-5	B-6	B-12	C	D	E	F	K	P
potato				x	x			x				x	
prunes	x	x	x	x		x							
pumpkin	x							x					
radishes	x							x					
raspberries								x					
rhubarb	x							x					
spinach	x		x					x		x	x	x	
sprouts, bean	x	x	x	x	x	x	x	x		x	x		
squash, wntr.	x		x					x					
strawberries		x	x									x	
sweet potato	x	x	x					x					
Swiss chard	x							x					
tangerine	x							x					
tomato	x				x			x					
turnip								x					
watercress	x		x					x					
watermelon	x							x					
wheatgrass	x	x	x	x	x	x	x	x		x	x	x	
zucchini	x	x	x					x					

APPENDIX E: MINERAL CONTENT OF PRODUCE

PRODUCE	calcium	iodine	iron	magnesium	phosphorus	potassium	sodium	zinc
alfalfa sprouts	X		X	X	X		X	X
apple		X		X		X	X	X
apricot	X		X	X	X	X		
artichoke	X		X		X	X	X	
asparagus		X	X		X		X	X
avocado				X		X		
banana			X	X	X	X		
beans, green	X	X	X		X	X	X	
beet greens	X				X	X	X	
beets		X	X	X	X	X	X	
bell pepper		X			X	X		
blackberries	X	X				X		
blueberries	X	X			X	X		
broccoli	X		X			X	X	
Brussels sprouts		X	X				X	

PRODUCE	calcium	iodine	iron	magnesium	phosphorus	potassium	sodium	zinc
cabbage	x	x			x		x	
cantaloupe					x	x	x	
carrot	x	x					x	
cauliflower	x							
celery	x	x			x		x	
cherries			x			x		
coconut	x	x		x	x			
collard greens	x	x					x	
corn				x	x			x
cranberries	x				x	x		
cucumber	x		x		x	x		
dates	x		x	x	x	x	x	
eggplant		x				x		
figs	x		x	x		x	x	
garlic		x		x	x		x	x
ginger root	x					x		x
grapefruit	x	x		x		x		
grapes	x		x	x	x	x		

PRODUCE	calcium	iodine	iron	magnesium	phosphorus	potassium	sodium	zinc
kale		X			X		X	X
lemon	X	X		X		X		
lettuce	X	X						X
lima beans	X	X						
lime	X	X			X	X		
mushroom								X
mustard greens	X	X			X	X	X	
okra	X		X	X	X	X		
onion	X				X	X	X	
orange	X	X				X		
papaya	X				X	X		
parsley	X		X	X	X		X	
parsnip	X				X	X		
peach				X				
pear	X	X		X	X	X	X	X
peas					X			
pineapple	X	X	X	X	X	X		
plum	X		X		X	X		

162   APPENDIX E: MINERAL CONTENT

PRODUCE	calcium	iodine	iron	magnesium	phosphorus	potassium	sodium	zinc
potato					X	X		
prunes	X		X	X		X	X	
pumpkin	X				X	X		
radishes	X				X	X		
raspberries	X		X		X	X		
rhubarb	X				X	X		
spinach		X	X				X	X
sprouts, bean	X		X	X	X	X	X	
squash, wntr.		X				X		
strawberries		X					X	
sweet potato	X	X						
Swiss chard		X	X		X		X	
tangerine		X				X		
tomato		X				X		
turnip	X	X				X		
watercress	X	X		X	X	X	X	
watermelon		X				X	X	
wheatgrass	X		X	X	X	X	X	X
zucchini	X				X	X		

APPENDIX F: NATURE'S PHARMACY

HEALTH PROBLEM	FOODS THAT MIGHT HELP
acne	apple, cantaloupe, carrot, cucumber, dale, strawberry
allergies	cantaloupe, cauliflower, garlic, kale, parsley, pepper, spinach
anemia	bean sprouts, beet, grape, plum, spinach, watercress
arthritis	broccoli, celery, grapefruit, pineapple, Swiss chard
asthma	broccoli, cranberry, collard greens
bladder infection	carrot, cranberry, cucumber, garlic, lemon, zucchini
bronchitis	broccoli, collard greens, garlic, lettuce, lemon, onion, parsley, pineapple, tomato, watermelon
cancer	apple, broccoli, carrot, cantaloupe, collard greens, garlic, kale, parsley, peppers, spinach, wheatgrass

HEALTH PROBLEM	FOODS THAT MIGHT HELP
candidiasis	beet greens, broccoli, carrot, garlic, ginger root, kale, parsley, radish, spinach
cholesterol	basil, cabbage, garlic, peppers, mint, parsley
chronic fatigue	bean sprouts, broccoli, carrot, cauliflower, garlic, ginger root, kale, parsley, peppers, potato, spinach
colitis	banana, blackberry, cabbage, carrot, corn, ginger root, parsley
colds	garlic, grapefruit, kale, lime, onion
constipation	grapefruit, rhubarb, spinach
depression	beet greens, broccoli, corn, garlic, kale, peppers, spinach
diabetes	avocado, blueberry, Brussels sprouts, corn, green beans, pear
diarrhea	apple, banana, beet, beet greens, blackberry, carrot
eczema	cabbage, carrot, cucumber, parsley, spinach, tomato
gout	broccoli, beet greens, cherry, horseradish, kale, parsley, peppers, pineapple, strawberry

HEALTH PROBLEM	FOODS THAT MIGHT HELP
hair loss	alfalfa sprouts, carrot, lettuce, parsley, spinach
headaches	apple, celery
herpes simplex	apple, blueberry, cantaloupe, carrot, ginger root, kale
hypoglycemia	apple, beet greens, carrot, peppers, spinach
indigestion	cabbage, carrot, papaya, peppers, pineapple
inflammation	ginger root, parsley, peppers, pineapple, watercress
insomnia	apple, blackberry, broccoli, celery, lettuce, pear
kidney problems	lemon, lettuce, pear, potato, tomato, zucchini
memory loss	asparagus, cantaloupe, carrot, kale, parsley, spinach
menstrual problems	beet greens, cabbage, collard greens, cucumber, grape, kale, okra, parsley, pineapple, tomato
migraines	collard greens, garlic, ginger root, parsley
overweight	celery, vegetable juices, drink juice before meals
psoriasis	cantaloupe, carrot, garlic, ginger root, parsley, papaya, pineapple
stress	beet, carrot, collard greens, lemon, lettuce, parsley, spinach, Swiss chard
ulcers	banana, cabbage, cantaloupe, carrot, celery, peppers

HEALTH PROBLEM	FOODS THAT MIGHT HELP
underweight	apple, cantaloupe, carrot, grape, pineapple, lemon, drink juices after meals
varicose veins	berries, cherry, garlic, ginger root, onion, pineapple
water retention	asparagus, bean sprouts, cucumber, parsley, watermelon

INDEX

Grapefruit
  ginger sorbet 87
  juice 6, 21, 24, 87, 109
  pineapple punch 24
Green bean juice 17
Green bell pepper
  juice 17, 22
  pulp 44, 130
Growing season of produce 149
Guacamole sauce 48
Guava juice 7

Health problems 164-167
Honey curry glaze 51

Iron builder 14

Jelly
  apple 63
  lime 62
  zucchini 64
Juice yields 146-148

Kaanipali sauce 43
Kale juice 19, 20

Lemon
  angel whispers 124
  chicken soup 30
  chiffon pie 115

cream cheese muffins 110
custard glaze 60
juice 5, 8, 15, 23, 29, 30, 32, 39,
  40, 41, 47, 48, 50, 51, 53, 60,
  63, 64, 67, 71, 72, 73, 76, 77,
  80, 81, 83, 84, 85, 86, 89, 90,
  91, 92, 94, 97 100, 105, 106,
  109, 110, 111, 113, 115, 121,
  124, 133, 134, 135, 138, 139,
  140, 143
lime pie 91
meringue pie 105
pepper chicken 133
prawn soup 29
risotto 143
sherbet 90
snow 94
soufflé, chilled 92
tarts 113
walnut bread 97
Lettuce juice 12, 15, 18
Lime
  butter sauce 42
  cake 120
  chutney chicken salad 75
  jelly 62
  juice 29, 30, 40, 42, 44, 45, 57,
    62, 75, 120, 134
  sauce 57

Mango
  pulp 41
  sauce 41
Mediterranean green beans 139
Mineral content of produce 160
Mock spinach soufflé 140
Moist apple cake 102
Molded fruit salad 70
Molded lime salad 66
Monday morning tonic 17
Muffins, lemon cream cheese 110

Nature's pharmacy 164-167

Onion
  juice 19
  pulp 33, 34, 39, 40, 43, 48, 49,
    50, 72, 74, 77, 79, 108, 130,
    131, 133, 136, 143, 144, 145

Orange
  cake, fresh 98
  caramel sauce 61
  cheesecake 103
  chiffon cake 116
  date bars 123
  dressing 79
  French toast 126
  glaze 38